Sylvia's Wedding

A play

Jimmie Chinn

Samuel French — London
New York - Toronto - Hollywood

Copyright © 1996 Jimmie Chinn
All Rights Reserved

SYLVIA'S WEDDING is fully protected under the copyright laws of the British Commonwealth, including Canada, the United States of America, and all other countries of the Copyright Union. All rights, including professional and amateur stage productions, recitation, lecturing, public reading, motion picture, radio broadcasting, television and the rights of translation into foreign languages are strictly reserved.

ISBN 978-0-573-01873-2

www.samuelfrench.co.uk
www.samuelfrench.com

For Amateur Production Enquiries

United Kingdom and World
excluding north america

plays@SamuelFrench-London.co.uk

020 7255 4302/01

Each title is subject to availability from Samuel French,

depending upon country of performance.

CAUTION: Professional and amateur producers are hereby warned that SYLVIA'S WEDDING is subject to a licensing fee. Publication of this play does not imply availability for performance. Both amateurs and professionals considering a production are strongly advised to apply to the appropriate agent before starting rehearsals, advertising, or booking a theatre. A licensing fee must be paid whether the title is presented for charity or gain and whether or not admission is charged.

The professional rights in this play are controlled by Samuel French Ltd, 52 Fitzroy Street, London, W1T 5JR

No one shall make any changes in this title for the purpose of production. No part of this book may be reproduced, stored in a retrieval system, or transmitted in any form, by any means, now known or yet to be invented, including mechanical, electronic, photocopying, recording, videotaping, or otherwise, without the prior written permission of the publisher. No one shall upload this title, or part of this title, to any social media websites.

The right of Jimmie Chinn to be identified as author of this work has been asserted in accordance with Section 77 of the Copyright, Designs and Patents Act 1988.

SYLVIA'S WEDDING

First presented at Oldham Coliseum on 16th March, 1995 with the following cast:

Yvonne	Sally Ann Matthews
Joyce	Pauline Jefferson
Vic	Norman Rossington
Sylvia	Lynette McMorrough
Stanley	Frederick Pyne
Myrtle	Penny Leatherbarrow
Gordon	Robert Hudson

Directed by Warren Hooper
Designed by Keith Orton
Lighting by Phil Clarke and Nicky Patterson
Sound by Sharon Nokes

CHARACTERS

Yvonne, *32*
Joyce, *50s-60s*
Vic, *Joyce's husband, 50s-60s*
Sylvia, *Vic's and Joyce's daughter, 32*
Stanley, *50s-60s*
Myrtle, *Stanley's wife, 50s-60s*
Gordon, *Myrtle's and Stanley's son, 32*

The action of the play takes place in a small end-of-terrace house

Time: Not so long ago ...

SYNOPSIS OF SCENES

ACT I

SCENE 1: Valentine's Night. The Engagement
SCENE 2: A Month Later. The Preparations

ACT II

SCENE 1: The Night Before
SCENE 2: The Big Day

Other plays by Jimmie Chinn published by
Samuel French Ltd

**After September
Albert Make Us Laugh
But Yesterday
From Here to the Library
Home Before Dark,** *or*, **The Saga of Miss Edie Hill
In By The Half
In Room Five Hundred and Four
Interior Designs
Pity About Kitty
A Respectable Funeral
Something To Remember You By
Straight and Narrow
Take Away the Lady
Too Long an Autumn**

For Lynette — love J.C.

ACT I

Scene 1

Valentine's Night: The Engagement

A small, end-of-terrace house. Night

The front door of the house — number 33 — is R. *In front of the house, part of a small front garden is visible, with a low wall; beyond the door is a small hallway where we can see the foot of a flight of stairs and a small table with a telephone. Doors lead from the hallway to the living-room* R, *which constitutes the main acting area, and to a smaller kitchen* L. *Cutaway walls should be used to increase the visibility of the hall and kitchen. A back door with a frosted glass panel leads from the kitchen into a small garden, which is visible through the kitchen window and also accessible via an alley leading from the front garden around the back of the house*

The living-room has a sofa, coffee table, armchair and TV set downstage, a sideboard and a budgie cage upstage; the kitchen has the usual sink, kitchen units, oven, fridge etc. ... and, prominently, a table and chairs

As the play begins, it is night, and raining. The house interior is in darkness. A street lamp sheds its light over the front garden

Joyce and Vic are in the living-room, facing the television, Joyce watching, Vic half asleep in his chair

Yvonne enters from the street wearing her dressing gown, bedroom slippers and holding up a small umbrella to protect her hair which is in rollers. She tries the front door of number 33 and finds it shut, so goes round the side of the house and disappears

The Lights come up slowly on the living-room; the television flickers over Joyce and Vic

Yvonne enters the kitchen from the back door, closing her umbrella

As Yvonne enters, the Lights come up on the kitchen

Yvonne (*calling*) It's only me, Mrs Lomax.
Joyce (*engrossed in the telly*) You what, love?
Yvonne (*opening the fridge door*) I've run out of milk again.

Joyce (*calling*) Just a sec, love — I want to see if this woman's got cancer.
Yvonne (*taking a bottle of milk from the fridge and pouring some into a cup at the sink*) I don't know what it is with me and milk but I can't seem to judge it — I've either got two gallons of it all going sour or none at all.
Joyce (*calling*) Is that Yvonne? (*This is always pronounced "EEvonne"*)
Yvonne Yes, love, it's Yvonne. I'll only take half a cupful. Are you sure you can spare it?
Joyce (*about the television*) He'll be heartbroken when he discovers she hasn't long to live.
Yvonne (*replacing the milk bottle in the fridge*) It's just for a cup of tea tonight and me cornflakes in the morning. (*She heads for the living-room*)
Vic (*waking with a start*) Eh? Did somebody mention tea? I'm parched, Joyce.
Joyce Just shut it will you — can't you see I'm watching this?
Yvonne (*appearing at the living-room door, cup of milk in hand*) No Sylvia?
Joyce (*still glued to the television*) It's her night at the pictures with Gordon. (*Of the television*) Have you been watching this?
Yvonne (*coming into the room, eyes on the television*) No. I can't seem to take to it. It's her. She always looks as if a good wash wouldn't do her any harm.
Vic I said I'm parched here — I'm parched, Joyce.
Joyce You know where the kettle is: you plug it in, switch it on and it boils. (*Of the television*) Oh, look at her now — you can tell she's lost weight.
Yvonne You shouldn't leave that back door open, you know — not these days — I could have been anybody ...
Vic I'll start making me own tea; then see where it lands you. I'm not helpless, you know.
Joyce (*as the television programme ends*) Now, isn't that typical: get to the interesting bit and you have to wait till next week. I reckon she's going to die and they haven't been married twelve month. (*She belches slightly*) Oh, that frozen lasagne keeps repeating on me. (*She switches off the television*)
Vic That's right — shut it off now I want to watch something.
Joyce We're not having rotten football for the rest of the night, Vic, no way. All day Saturday's enough without having it rammed down our throats mid-week. (*She moves into the kitchen*) Will you have a cup of tea, Yvonne?
Yvonne No, thanks — I'll wait till I get home.
Vic I don't half fancy egg on toast, Joyce.
Joyce (*filling the kettle at the sink*) You'll get no egg on toast out of me tonight. It's not Joyce's Caff, you know. (*She looks in the kitchen mirror*) I'm sure this blemish on my face is getting worse — what do you reckon, Yvonne?
Yvonne What did the doctor say?

Act I, Scene 1 3

Joyce (*plugging in the kettle, etc..*) He says I'm all nerves and gave me some ointment but it's done no good. (*She takes a tablet with some water*)
Vic (*calling*) I'll keep the sound down low.
Joyce I've said no, Vic. You should have married a football, you!
Yvonne (*calling to Joyce*) Will you tell Sylvia I'll be late in work tomorrow — I've got a chap coming in to unblock my sink.
Vic (*picking up a newspaper*) I might as well get to bed at this rate, staring at a blank screen. It's me who pays for this telly, you know! (*He reads his paper during the following*)
Joyce (*setting cups etc. on a tray*) There's a nice play on at half-past — you can watch that. About this woman with no arms or legs.
Vic Sounds bloody cheerful, does that.
Joyce It's an award winner — based on actuality.
Vic (*to Yvonne*) Bloody weddings, funerals, cripples and cancer. That's all she ever watches.
Joyce (*calling to Yvonne as she works*) How's your Auntie Betty, Yvonne — have you heard?
Yvonne They're whipping her in tomorrow, doing the op on Friday and she should be home by Monday. They don't mess about these days. They dissolve it now, you know. Open you up, shove this thing in, sew you up and "how's-your-father". Mind you, they've told her she'll be off balance for a week or two.
Joyce (*looking in the mirror again*) I'll tell you what, I wish they could dissolve this blemish: I'd be in there like a shot.
Vic (*of the paper*) Have you seen this? I'll be next, mark my words: just see if I'm not.
Joyce (*entering the living-room carrying a tray of cups, etc.*) Oh, don't start on about all that again, Vic.
Vic This'll be me — redundant. On the scrap-heap at my age!
Joyce You'll not be redundant in this house. You've been going to mend that lavatory for the last six years.
Yvonne Is it on the cards then, Mr Lomax?
Vic If I don't get a letter in the next fortnight I'll be very lucky.
Joyce Just leave off about it, Vic. Yvonne doesn't want to hear all this. If you're redundified you're redundified. It won't kill you. (*She goes back to the kitchen*)
Vic (*calling*) You won't be saying that when there's no money coming in. No living it up then.
Joyce (*returning with milk, sugar, etc.*) We don't live it up now. We're stuck in this house seven nights a week. I just thank God our Sylvia's got a very active social life.
Yvonne Sylvia?
Joyce Well, at least she's got Gordon to see she gets a bit of pleasure.

Yvonne Pleasure! With Gordon? I get more pleasure Hoovering my back passage!
Joyce (*choosing to ignore this, going back to the kitchen*) Will you have a digestive or not, Vic?
Vic Have we nothing else?
Joyce Not in the biscuit line — no.
Vic I couldn't half go egg on toast, Joyce.
Joyce (*getting a tin of biscuits from a cupboard*) And I've told you once — if you want egg on toast you can do it yourself. I'm redundified tonight. Anyway, we've no bread till I go to the Centre tomorrow. (*She pours boiling water into the teapot*)
Vic I'm like a prisoner here. My own house and I can't have egg on toast when I fancy.

Sylvia comes round the corner and enters the garden from the street. She is dressed for a night at the pictures with a headscarf and an umbrella. She is holding a large pink envelope which contains a Valentine card. She fumbles for her door key and is about to open the front door but seems to have second thoughts; instead, she sits on the low garden wall, umbrella still up, and opens her card to read it once more

Joyce enters the living-room, carrying the teapot and the tin of biscuits

Joyce Anyway, he should look on the bright side, shouldn't he, Yvonne? You'll get a lump sum, Vic. That's what they do when they lay you off.
Yvonne How long have you been there, Mr Lomax?
Vic You know how long I've been there: all me bloody life, that's how long I've been there.
Yvonne There you are then, it should be quite a tidy nest egg.
Joyce Don't start him off on eggs again, Yvonne. (*She hands Vic his tea*) And don't spill it.
Yvonne All I'm saying, Mrs Lomax, is he's bound to get quite a few thousands if he's laid off.
Joyce There you are then. A few thousand should just see us through. (*She pours her own tea*)
Vic See me through! I don't want anything to "see me through", woman. I want to work till I'm sixty-five — not be cooped up here with you all day. It'd drive me mad.
Joyce I've told you: there's plenty here to keep you occupied. A washer on that bathroom tap for a start. That'll take you a week or two.
Vic That's right, be sarcastic.
Yvonne (*laughing*) I'm getting out of here before there's a row. (*She goes into the kitchen and collects her umbrella*)

Act I, Scene 1   5

Joyce (*sitting, tea in hand*) You could put up a new clothes line, paint the garden shed, sharpen your tools, lay a bit of lawn out there. Enough to keep you going till you're ninety.
Yvonne (*heading to the front door*) See you — thanks for the milk.
Vic Ninety! I'll be well under by then — thank God.
Joyce (*calling*) 'Night, Yvonne.

Yvonne opens the front door to leave and sees Sylvia still sitting on the wall

Yvonne Sylv. What you doing out here?
Sylvia Hallo, Yvonne. Run out of milk again?
Yvonne (*seeing the card*) What's that? I've not forgot your birthday again have I? (*She takes the card from Sylvia and reads*) "Roses are red, violets are blue, I'm yours forever but I mustn't say who!"
Sylvia It's a Valentine card, Yvonne.
Yvonne I can see what it is, Sylv.
Sylvia The first one I've ever had.
Yvonne Who's it from?
Sylvia You know who it's from. Gordon, of course.
Yvonne God — he took his time. You've been seeing him for ten years. Here, are you OK, Sylv?
Sylvia (*obviously in a slight daze*) I'm getting married, Yvonne.
Yvonne I'm sorry?
Sylvia Married. Me. Sylvia Lomax. I'm getting married.
Yvonne Who to?
Sylvia Oh, you are funny, Yvonne. Gordon. He finally asked me. Tonight. After the pictures. In the chippy as a matter of fact. "Cod and chips twice and a tub of curry sauce," I said to the woman — and that's when it happened. He gave me the Valentine's card and said, "We can't keep messing about," he said, "we might as well get married". He's gone home to tell his parents.
Yvonne (*almost to herself*) Oh, my God!
Sylvia I thought he was kidding — you know what his sense of humour's like — but the woman serving said, "Oh, it's your lucky night, love!" ... so I knew I wasn't dreaming. (*She takes her card back and re-reads it*)
Yvonne I think I need a drink, Sylv.
Sylvia That's the last thing I need — I'm all light-headed as it is. Were you all light-headed when Malcolm proposed to you?
Yvonne I was, love. But that was morning sickness; I was three months gone with our Roy. My second husband just said, "Get your knickers off and get up them stairs!" (*A beat. She looks at her friend almost sympathetically*) Hadn't we better go in, Sylv — it's perishing out here.
Sylvia Is it? I'm on cloud nine, Yvonne.

Yvonne Come on—I think you and I need to talk. (*She pushes the front door open to enter the house*) Just wait till your Mam hears this, eh?
Sylvia I don't think it's wise to tell her just yet. You know what she is about weddings; it'll set her off.
Yvonne She'll have to know sometime, Sylv.
Sylvia Later, eh? When I'm ready.

They enter the house, closing the door behind them. They head for the kitchen

The Lights go down on the garden

Joyce (*to Vic*) Anyway, you could get a little part-time job like Cyril.
Vic Oh, yes?
Joyce Zebra crossing, handyman: something like that. According to Ivy, Cyril's never been happier. He's got his little stall on the market.
Sylvia (*passing the living-room door*) Hallo, Mum, hallo, Dad. I'm back.
Joyce Hallo, love.
Vic Selling what?
Yvonne (*as she passes the living-room door*) I'm back; I just want a word with your Sylvia.

Sylvia and Yvonne enter the kitchen and close the door slightly. Yvonne fills a glass with water from the tap

Joyce He sells knick-knacks.
Vic Knick-knacks. What bloody knick-knacks?
Joyce I don't know. Ivy said knick-knacks. At least he's occupied, at least he's out of trouble. Keep your eye on that clock.

They fall silent

Yvonne (*handing Sylvia the glass of water*) Here, drink this. Shall I run over and get you one of my tablets?
Sylvia I don't need a tablet, Yvonne. I'm fine.
Yvonne Well, I'm not. (*She gulps the water down*) Oh, Sylv.
Sylvia (*sitting at the table*) What d'you mean, "Oh, Sylv"?
Yvonne (*sitting opposite her*) I suppose you've said yes.
Sylvia Of course I've said yes. It's all I've ever wanted, Yvonne. To marry Gordon.
Yvonne But why? You're perfectly happy as you are. Once a week the pictures, once a fortnight *Romeo and Juliet's*, then he goes home to Myrtle and Stanley — bliss, Sylv. Why have him under your feet twenty-four hours a day?

Act I, Scene 1 7

Sylvia Look, Yvonne, I'm sorry, I know you've never liked Gordon but you are supposed to be my best friend, you know.
Yvonne I am. I am your best friend. That's why I want you to be happy.
Sylvia But I will be happy. Gordon and I were meant for each other.
Yvonne (*rising*) I'm going to get you a cup of tea. That's what you need — a cup of tea with plenty of sugar. (*She goes to the living-room*)
Sylvia (*calling*) No sugar. I'm giving it up from now on.
Yvonne (*entering the living-room*) She'd like a cup of tea, Mrs Lomax. (*She picks up the teapot and pours a cup of tea during the following*)
Joyce Is she all right?
Yvonne She's fine. Feeling a bit bilious, I think. (*She returns to the kitchen*)
Joyce 'Flu, I expect — she has been looking peaky all week. (*She calls*) Tell her to take a Lemsip with an aspirin in it, Yvonne.
Vic (*picking up the biscuit from his saucer*) Not bloody digestive again.
Joyce There's folk in foreign parts who'd give their right arm for a digestive biscuit.
Sylvia (*to Yvonne who is pouring tea*) We thought Easter Saturday — so put it in your diary. The weather should be fine by then; and a honeymoon in Fleetwood — we love Fleetwood — and they say it's become ever so popular again.
Yvonne (*to heaven*) I don't believe this — I don't. (*She gives the tea to Sylvia*) Here, drink this and shut it. (*She sits at the table, taking Sylvia's hand*) Look, Sylvia, I just want you to think about this. Think, love.
Sylvia I'm all of a shake, Yvonne.
Yvonne I can see.
Sylvia So many things rushing through my mind. I mean, how d'you think Mum a' Dad'll take it?
Yvonne I'm not bothered about them — it's you I'm concerned about.
Sylvia But they do take me for granted, Yvonne, you know that. They always have. I've often thought that if I went missing it'd be at least a fortnight before they noticed.
Yvonne Now, that's not true. They'd fall apart without you.
Sylvia That's what worries me. I mean, how would they manage: I've kept them going really, haven't I?
Yvonne (*slightly moved by her friend*) Course you have, love.
Sylvia But I can't let that interfere, can I? And after all, I am adopted, aren't I, I'm not actually their daughter, am I?
Yvonne Well, no, but they did fetch you up, Sylv. They have looked after you for thirty years.
Sylvia Yes, but they should have *told* me.
Yvonne They did, Sylv — they did tell you.
Sylvia Yes, eventually. When I was twenty-seven! And only then because I needed my birth certificate to get a passport!

Yvonne Forget it, Sylv. That's all in the past.
Sylvia So why should I be worried about telling them I'm getting married? (*A fresh worry now*) And what's Gordon going to say when I tell him I'm illegitimate?
Yvonne Don't tell him. It's none of his business.
Sylvia But what if his parents find out? You know the Broadbents: everything on the level, everything above board.
Yvonne Oh, sod the Broadbents! Who cares about the Broadbents?
Sylvia (*reassured, smiling*) You're right, Yvonne. I'm worrying too much, aren't I?
Yvonne Well, I wouldn't say that, Sylv. There are some things to think about, love. The wedding: who's going to pay for that?
Sylvia Oh, we don't want anything fancy. Something simple. A registry office, cheese on sticks, a piece of cream sponge: that'll suit us, Yvonne.
Yvonne And a place to live, Sylv. You'll need somewhere to live — it all needs thinking about.
Sylvia You're trying to put me off, aren't you?
Yvonne I'm not, Sylv — honest.
Sylvia I know you, Yvonne, you're trying to say it isn't a good idea. Well, I'm not going to listen, it's all settled and that's that!

Joyce leaves the living-room and appears at the kitchen door

Joyce What's all settled? What am I missing?
Yvonne Oh, it's something and nothing, Mrs Lomax. We were just discussing work, that's all. Weren't we, Sylv?

Joyce gets bird seed etc. from a cupboard and fills a small jug with water at the tap

Joyce I'd better just put Hoppy to bed before the play starts.

Sylvia and Yvonne exchange glances

Vic (*taking another biscuit: to himself*) Bloody digestive; I mean, if she got chocolate digestive at least it'd be a change!
Joyce Did I tell you I got another of those funny 'phone calls, Yvonne?
Yvonne (*not really listening*) You should ring the police, Mrs Lomax. I know I would.

During the following dialogue, Joyce takes the bird seed etc. through to the living-room where she gives the budgie more seed and fresh water, then covers it with a cloth with the word "Hoppy" embroidered on it

Act I, Scene 1

Joyce It turned my stomach, I can tell you. (*She calls to the bird*) Bedtime, Hoppy-Whoppy!
Vic (*to himself*) That bird gets more attention than I do!

Yvonne gives Sylvia a pat on the hand and comes through to the living-room with her cup of milk and her umbrella

Joyce (*as she works at the bird cage*) Yes, this voice said, "Mrs Lomax?", I said "Yes" ... "Mrs Joyce Lomax?" ...
Yvonne (*sitting on the arm of the sofa*) He knew your name then?
Joyce "Yes", I said, "this is Mrs Joyce Lomax, how can I help you?" I said. "I'm delighted to inform you", he says, "that you are the lucky winner of our weekly prize". "Oh", I said, "what's that?" He said, "You have won a complete set of the latest Paris underwear in either off-white satin or sheer black nylon, which would you prefer?" (*To the bird*) Mummy's giving you fresh seed and water, Hoppy — yes! "Off white satin sounds nice", I said, "I'm a bit too old for sheer black nylon." "How old are you?" he said. So I told him and I thought it was odd then because he said, "Oh, I prefer the more mature woman any day."
Vic Perverts. You can spot 'em a mile off.
Joyce "Could you give me your bra size?" he said — so I did — then he said, "Would you prefer the scanty-panty or the garment for the fuller figure?"
Yvonne I'd have put the phone down, wouldn't you, Mr Lomax?
Vic He never rings me.
Joyce "I like my knickers up to my waist," I said and that's when I fell in — he started breathing heavily. "You sound as if you suffer from asthma", I said. Then, and without any prior warning, he said something quite obscene. I put the phone down then, I can tell you! (*She covers the cage with the cloth*) Good-night, sweetheart. Say good-night, Yvonne.
Yvonne 'Night, Hoppy.
Joyce (*calling*) Sylv ...
Sylvia (*still at the kitchen table*) Good-night, Hoppy.
Joyce (*sharply*) Vic — say good-night to this bird.
Vic (*looking to heaven*) Good-night, Hoppy.
Yvonne Right, well, I'd best be off, back to my virgin couch — thank God! (*She rises to leave*)
Joyce (*lowering her voice*) How's she?
Yvonne She's fine. (*She calls*) Aren't you, Sylv? She's a lot on her mind, that's all. (*She heads towards the front door, calling*) Oh, I'll be late in tomorrow, Sylv, I'm getting my sink unblocked. Ta-ra!

Yvonne comes out of the house, shuts the door and exits to the street

Joyce moves into the kitchen and starts washing up, etc.

Joyce Did you have your period, Sylv?
Sylvia It came this afternoon. While I was on me tea-break so I was lucky.
Joyce Still, it's not right, four days late like that: I'd have a word with Doctor Tweedale if I were you.
Sylvia I think it's all these vitamins I'm taking. They've sent my whole system hectic.
Joyce Lot on your mind, have you, love?
Sylvia Oh, this an' that — you know.
Joyce Never mind, it'll soon be the wedding.
Sylvia (*startled*) What wedding ...?
Joyce Your cousin Julie's, a week on Saturday.
Sylvia Oh, that.
Joyce I thought I'd wear something mauveish — what d'you think?
Sylvia Oh, not mauveish, Mum. Very funereal is mauve. How about green? Now green is a very nice colour.
Joyce Very unlucky though, Sylv. Look at Mavis Leadbetter — she wore green to that dinner-dance at the Town Hall and she's been on a life support machine ever since. (*She heads back to the living-room*) There's a nice play on at half-past — that'll cheer you up, Sylv.
Sylvia (*wanting to tell her now*) Mum ...
Joyce (*not listening, entering the living-room*) Did I tell you Barry Bingley got run over? There's no guarantee he'll ever walk again.

Sylvia, looking slightly lost, follows her mother into the living-room and sits beside her on the sofa

He's been staying in Abu Dhabi at an inter-continental hotel. Safe as houses. Comes home and gets run over outside the Halifax. You never know, do you? (*She switches on the television with the sound off*) Right — everybody cosy?
Vic I'm not sitting here watching hospital stuff, Joyce.
Joyce Who said it's hospital stuff? It's not hospital stuff. It has nothing to do with hospitals.

Silence

Sylvia Gordon said I had breasts like Dolly Parton tonight, Dad.
Vic (*reading his paper*) She's a big bugger she is.
Sylvia I suppose I am a bit overweight, Mum — what d'you think?
Vic Overweight! I'd have said you were fat, Sylvia.
Joyce (*throwing a cushion at him*) Vic!
Vic Well, she asked, didn't she?

They each fall silent, gazing at the soundless television screen

Act I, Scene 1   11

The Lights come up on the garden

Stanley, Myrtle and Gordon enter from the street

Stanley Now just leave all this to me, Myrtle. Don't go opening your mouth — right?
Myrtle Yes, well just be careful what you're saying, Stanley — we don't want a row.
Sylvia (*bracing herself again*) Mum ... Dad ...
Joyce Yes, love ...

Stanley rings the doorbell; it is loud

Vic Who the hell's that at this time of night? Ignore it, Joyce.
Gordon Shall I wait out here?
Stanley What d'you want to wait out here for? I want you in there, lad. (*He looks up at the house*) They're not in bed are they?
Sylvia (*worried*) Shall I go?
Vic You stop where you are. It might be somebody canvassing.
Joyce Canvassing. Canvassing for what?
Vic How do I know? Just keep quiet and pretend to be out.
Joyce How can we pretend to be out? Every light in the house is on. Talk sense.
Vic Well, I'm not putting my shirt on. I don't care who it is.
Stanley Shall I go round the back?
Myrtle You can't do that. It's private.
Stanley Well, I'm not standing here all night. (*He bangs loudly on the door knocker*)
Sylvia They're very persistent whoever it is. It wouldn't be the police would it?
Joyce Oh, don't say that, Sylv. My stomach's going over as it is.
Stanley (*shouting through the letter box*) We know you're in there — open this door!
Myrtle Stan! You'll have the neighbours out.
Stanley Hard luck, Myrtle. We want this settled tonight. (*He shouts through the letter box again*) It's us. Mr and Mrs Broadbent and son Gordon — it's no use hiding!
Gordon (*embarrassed, sitting on the wall*) Dad!
Sylvia Oh, my God — it's Gordon with his mum and dad.
Joyce I do hope there's not been a tragedy. You'd better go, Vic.
Vic I'm stopping where I am. What do they want at this time of night? Sylvia, have you been up to something? (*During the following he changes the television channel and starts to watch the football*)

Stanley I'll smash a window in a minute.
Myrtle Just calm down, Stanley. Gordon, have you not got a special signal or something?
Gordon How d'you mean?
Myrtle Well, a special way of knocking. To let them know it's you.
Gordon (*puzzled*) No.
Joyce My nerves won't stand this; I'm going. (*She rises, goes out into the hall and opens the front door*)
Stanley Oh. At last. We thought you'd flitted.
Joyce We were just about to have our bedtime beverage, Mr Broadbent. We thought there was a fire.
Stanley A fire. Take more than a fire to shift you lot by the looks of it.
Myrtle Stan! Good-evening, Mrs Lomax. We thought we'd just pop round — you know how it is.
Joyce What for? It's nearly lights out in this house.
Gordon Can't we come tomorrow, Dad?
Stanley No, we can't. We've come tonight. Is your husband in?
Joyce Yes. But I'm afraid he's only got his vest on.
Stanley Never mind his vest. It's not his vest we've come to see. (*He pushes past Joyce*)
Joyce (*to Myrtle*) What on earth's it all about: is there a hoo-hah?
Myrtle I'm afraid Stanley will make a hoo-hah out of anything. (*She goes into the house*) Come along, Gordon: this is all your doing.
Gordon I'm sorry, Mrs Lomax — it's all a bit of a storm in a teacup I'm afraid.

Gordon goes into the house. Joyce looks out to see if any neighbours are watching, then goes in and closes the door

Stanley enters the living-room

Stanley (*removing his hat*) God! Is there a funny smell in here?
Vic Ay — you!
Stanley (*not hearing this, spotting Sylvia*) Ahh, so there you are. Miss Free-'n'-easy!
Sylvia Pardon?
Stanley Beneath that plump and pink exterior lies a bit of a ruthless streak I suppose.
Sylvia I don't know what you mean, Mr Broadbent. What does he mean, Dad?
Vic (*glued to the football match*) Don't ask me — I'm keeping out of it.
Myrtle Now, I hope you're not losing your temper, Stanley.

Joyce and Gordon enter the living-room. Gordon moves to stand behind Vic's armchair and they both become engrossed in the football match

Act I, Scene 1   13

Stanley Is this girl of yours still a virgin: that's what we'd like to know.
Sylvia That's a very personal question, Mr Broadbent. Gordon, what does all this mean?
Joyce Shall I put the kettle on?
Stanley We want no kettles on, thank you. We want some straight answers to some straight questions, don't we, Myrtle?
Sylvia I don't know what you're on about, Mr Broadbent. Gordon, what's your father on about, please?
Stanley I return from a heavy day in Skegness — a very busy day in Skegness, I might add — and what am I greeted with?
Myrtle (*to Joyce*) He wouldn't touch his supper.
Stanley News like this!
Joyce I'm sorry, we've no idea what you mean, have we, Victor? What news?
Stanley All we want to know is: is this daughter of yours up the spout?
Myrtle Stanley! Now that's enough! You're being unspeakably rude to these people. Just say: is your Sylvia with child — pregnant?
Sylvia All this is giving me a headache, Mum.
Stanley Are you having my son's child, young woman?
Sylvia (*almost in tears*) No!

Vic turns the TV sound up loud: obviously a goal is scored

Vic
Gordon } (*together*) Yeah!!!
Vic That goalie's a wanker!
Joyce Victor! Have some manners. Turn that sound down.

Vic turns the TV sound down

Perhaps Mr and Mrs Broadbent would like to see the news.
Sylvia What's this all about, Gordon?
Gordon (*without taking his eyes off the screen*) Search me. I just told him about us and he went mad.
Joyce (*to Myrtle*) I could do you a nice egg on toast, only I've no bread: sorry.
Stanley I'm not having my son tricked into marrying the first woman who comes along. There's too much at stake.
Joyce I could manage some cream crackers with cheese.
Myrtle (*to Joyce*) You see, we've no objection to our Gordon seeing your Sylvia but we'd never envisaged marriage. We've never considered marriage as being on the cards, have we, Stanley?
Stanley Have you been to bed with this young woman or not, Gordon?
Gordon No, course I haven't. Me an' Sylv aren't like that.
Stanley Then why in the name of all that's wonderful do you want to marry her?

Joyce (*delighted*) Does he? Oh, Sylv — it's your dream come true is this.
Sylvia Obviously, Mr and Mrs Broadbent don't agree. Obviously, they don't think I'm good enough to marry Gordon.
Joyce She doesn't always look like this, you know. She can look ever so smart when her hair's tinted and her nails are done, can't you, Sylv?

Sylvia is by now very upset. She rises in tears and goes out and into the kitchen where she sits at the table and just stares into space

Victor. Can you hear all this?

There is no reply

Victor, I shan't tell you again — turn that telly off now!

Vic, grunting, switches off the TV

Stanley There's no television in our house after ten o'clock at night, is there, Myrtle? We go to bed with Radio Four.
Myrtle (*to Joyce*) He likes to hear the shipping forecast.
Joyce Well, we only watch if there's a nice play on usually.
Stanley So, if your Sylvia's pregnant it's not by my son. Right, Gordon?

Gordon simply looks to heaven for support

Joyce Well, we didn't know she was pregnant, did we, Vic? Mind you — she was four days late with her period.
Stanley There you are then: living proof. There's no fooling nature!
Joyce She's always been very secretive with us. She never told us when the Gas Board promoted her. I just went in one day and there she was: a senior sales executive and everything.
Stanley Never mind all that now. I'm not prepared to stand by and watch my only son and heir being conned. I've seen too much of it.
Gordon I'm not being conned, Dad. Talk sense.
Joyce Can I take your coats?
Stanley No, thanks — we shan't be stopping.
Joyce Horlicks perhaps? I believe we have some left; we very rarely touch it.
Stanley Mrs Lomax, once and for all we are not here to socialize, nor to consume great quantities of Horlicks; we're here to establish what men your Sylvia is seeing on the nights when she doesn't see our Gordon.
Gordon Give it a rest, Dad — she isn't seeing anybody.
Stanley How do you know? Some women are capable of anything, lad — including two-timing!

Gordon Can't we go home now?
Stanley You'll go home when I'm good and ready. You'll let anybody twist you round their little finger, you. Honestly, at times you act like some bloody great nancy!
Myrtle There's no need to swear, Stanley. I'm not having that.
Stanley (*to Joyce*) Has she always been promiscuous?
Joyce (*lost*) Sorry?
Stanley Your daughter.
Joyce Well, yes, but she is taking vitamins for it.
Stanley There you are, Gordon — and this woman's her mother.
Gordon She's not promiscuous, Dad. I have been going out with her for ten years, you know.
Stanley What — every night of the week?
Gordon Well no. Once a week the pictures, once a fortnight *Romeo and Juliet's*.
Stanley Yes, and God alone knows what goes on in that place.
Gordon Old Tyme Dancing, that's all.
Stanley Yes, and drugs being peddled in the toilets I'll be bound.
Gordon What's he on about, Mum? Tell him will you.
Myrtle Just listen to your father, Gordon — he's a man of the world.
Stanley How do we know she's not sneaking off to some den of vice every night — what proof have we?
Joyce She's usually in bed by ten, isn't she, Victor?
Vic How long are they staying? I've got to get up for work in the morning.
Stanley Well, I'm sorry but I need this sorted out. My son's going to be a very wealthy young man when I'm dead and buried.
Myrtle Oh, don't talk like that, Stanley. (*To Joyce*) I hate it when he talks like that.
Joyce (*aside to Myrtle*) Cancer is it?
Stanley And he'll inherit my deckchair business. That involves a lot of entertaining. He needs a wife who can supervize the odd cocktail party, who's clean in her habits and from a respectable family, a personable manner on the telephone and with a knowledge of VAT. Not some fly-by-night who has the milkman in when her husband's back is turned!
Vic Here, hang on a minute.
Joyce Vic, keep out of this.
Vic This is us he's talking about — us and our Sylvia.
Joyce I'm warning you ...
Vic (*to Stanley*) And if you must know, our Sylvia's very good at VAT.
Joyce That's right — she was in the accounts department before they made her an executive.
Stanley (*looking suddenly uncomfortable*) Excuse me, have you a toilet?
Joyce (*ashen*) Sorry?

Stanley A toilet, a lavatory.
Joyce (*worried*) Well, yes. But the flushing device is a bit wonky, Mr Broadbent.
Stanley (*rushing out of the room*) Upstairs, I suppose.

Stanley exits up the stairs

Joyce (*quietly to Vic*) You see. I knew the day would come. Strangers in our toilet! (*She stands at the doorway, listening*)

Vic starts to fall asleep again during the following

Gordon Dad can be a right pain when he wants.
Myrtle He's only got your good at heart, Gordon. Some lads would give their eye teeth to have a father like yours.
Gordon I wish I'd never started all this. (*He moves towards the front door*) I'm going out for some fresh air.
Myrtle (*upset*) Now don't do anything hasty, Gordon.

Gordon goes through the front door into the garden where he sits quietly on the wall

Joyce (*trying to comfort Myrtle*) Children, eh? They're a problem from cradle to grave.
Myrtle I'm sorry about my husband — it's just the way he's made.
Joyce I know. (*She indicates Vic*) He can be the same.
Myrtle And he has this affliction. He's got to go every half-hour when he's in this mood.
Joyce I understand. I've seen it on the telly. His bowels I expect.
Myrtle Well, no ...
Joyce Will you have a soft drink, Mrs Broadbent?
Myrtle (*unbuttoning her coat*) If it's no trouble. It is rather warm in here.
Joyce We have to keep it an even temperature because of Hoppy. He's used to a tropical climate, you see.
Myrtle Hoppy?
Joyce In the cage. He'll have dropped off by now but why not take a peek? He won't bite — we've trained him.

Joyce leaves and goes into the kitchen where Sylvia is still at the table. Myrtle, meanwhile, goes over to the birdcage, gingerly lifts the cover and peers underneath it

(*Going to the fridge*) Oh, Sylvia, I never thought you'd let us down like this. (*She gets a carton of orange juice out of the fridge, and a glass,*

napkin and tray, etc.) Your dad in a dirty vest, Mr Broadbent struggling in our toilet — and now you in this condition.
Sylvia I am not pregnant, Mum.
Joyce And why didn't you tell us you were getting married? We'd have understood. It was so embarrassing.
Sylvia Well, it looks as if I'm not now, doesn't it? They say happiness is only fleeting, don't they? Well, it's certainly fleeted out of here quick enough.
Joyce Never mind — I'm sure it'll sort itself out.
Sylvia I really thought my turn had come, Mum. I did. A nice wedding, quiet with just one or two friends; a flat perhaps to start us off, then a little two-up two-down before settling into a well-appointed bungalow in our twilight years. It's not much to ask out of life is it?
Joyce It's really affected your dad. He doesn't say much but I know when he's shattered.

Vic snores in the other room. Myrtle jumps, fearing the budgie might escape and attack her

Joyce Is it all my fault, Sylv? Have I been a bad mother?
Sylvia I shall have to leave the Gas Showrooms now. I shan't be able to hold my head up; I'll be a laughing stock, an outcast, the girl who never quite made it.
Joyce Help yourself to juice if you fancy — I daren't keep her ladyship waiting.

Joyce makes her way back to the living-room and enters bearing the tray with a glass of juice and a napkin

Myrtle This bird has only one leg, Mrs Lomax.
Joyce I know. Proper tragedy really. That's why we call him Hoppy. It was all my fault. I'd left the back door open, he was out of his cage, out he flew, straight into the jaws of next-door's cat. I had to land out with the brush. We don't let him out now.
Myrtle It must have been a terrible ordeal for you.
Joyce Yes, but that's cats for you, they just see a good meal I suppose. (*She proffers the tray*) Orange. I usually have a choice but it's my day at the shops tomorrow.
Myrtle (*taking the glass*) I do apologize for all this, Mrs Lomax. (*Asking to sit down*) May I — do you mind?
Joyce No, please, make yourself at home.
Myrtle Men, eh? They will interfere. Never happier than when they're upsetting everything. (*She sits on the sofa*)
Joyce (*sitting beside her*) I know. He can be just the same. I'm sorry he's asleep but he's up at five every morning.

Myrtle Something big in the Post Office, did Gordon tell me?
Joyce Well, he's at the Post Office but I don't think he's anything big, Mrs Broadbent — he's a postman.
Myrtle I see. Now, what are we going to do about all this, Mrs Lomax?
Joyce About what?
Myrtle This. Our Gordon and your Sylvia.
Joyce She's a good girl really.
Myrtle I know she is, Mrs Lomax: anybody in their right mind can see that and I know our Gordon's quite devoted to her in his own way, but it's Stanley — he just went up the wall.
Joyce He seems dead set against it, doesn't he?
Myrtle Yes, and I can't think why. Doesn't he see this might be Gordon's only chance?
Joyce Sorry?
Myrtle Well, you know what I mean: Gordon and Sylvia are obviously very suited — same temperament and everything — and, let's face it, Mrs Lomax, neither of them are getting any younger, are they?
Joyce I suppose not.
Myrtle You see, working for his father's made him, well, reserved, awkward perhaps, shy almost. Of course, he's different again when he's got his football and his swimming, but at home, at work under his father, and here with your Sylvia he's, well ... you must have noticed.
Joyce He never says much, that's true.
Myrtle No, I think he's found the perfect partner in your Sylvia.
Joyce And she in him, Mrs Broadbent. She's never been out-going — her key's in that door on the dot — and she's a proper little home-maker. You should taste her chips.
Myrtle We could give them a fabulous wedding, couldn't we?
Vic (*waking up*) We've no money for weddings in this house!
Joyce Just shut it, Vic! She's our daughter; we can afford to see her married off.

In the garden, Gordon blows his nose. Then he enters the house, closing the door behind him

Vic picks up the paper and starts to read again

Myrtle She could wear my wedding dress — that'd cut the cost, Mr Lomax. It's still hanging in my wardrobe, good as new.
Joyce Oh, Vic — isn't it exciting?
Myrtle Of course, I'd have to alter it to fit her, put a piece in the back an' that — your Sylvia being on the biggish side.
Joyce Oh, she'll look a picture, Vic.

Act I, Scene 1

Myrtle I could make the bridesmaids' dresses. And do the catering. I'm an expert in the kitchen.

Gordon appears in the kitchen. Sylvia, still upset, ignores him

Myrtle Nothing's impossible, Mrs Lomax.
Joyce (*looking up at the ceiling*) Yes, but what about Mr Broadbent, what about him?
Myrtle (*also looking up*) Don't worry — I have my methods. (*With deeper meaning*) He'll go to Skegness once too often ...

The Lights fade slightly on the living-room and come up more intensely on the kitchen. Sylvia and Gordon are silent for a moment

Gordon (*after the pause*) Can I get a drink of water?
Sylvia (*refusing to look at him*) Get what you like.

Gordon gets a glass, fills it with water from the tap and drinks it in silence

(*Eventually*) This is the worst night of my life, Gordon.
Gordon Yes. (*He drinks again*)
Sylvia I caught a glimpse of paradise in that chip-shop this evening — but now, back to square one.
Gordon It'll all blow over, Sylv — it usually does.
Sylvia I've seen another side of you tonight, Gordon — a side I hadn't realized existed.
Gordon Oh?
Sylvia I've only ever seen your strength, your determination. Once a week at the pictures, dancing cheek-to-cheek once a fortnight at *Romeo and Juliet's*, swimming in your galas, playing football with your mates on a Sunday. But tonight, in front of your parents, you changed, Gordon.
Gordon I'm sorry.
Sylvia It's no use being sorry, Gordon. Your father was very rude to me in there. He said some unforgivable things.
Gordon He didn't mean them. You take everything too much to heart, Sylvia.
Sylvia He more or less accused me of being a tart, Gordon. Said I was pregnant when I'm not. You always said they liked me.
Gordon They do. Dad's had a bad day, that's all. He's always tetchy when he can't sell our deckchairs.
Sylvia Whole days go by sometimes and I don't sell any gas ovens, but it doesn't send me into a flying rage. I don't come round your house ranting and raving, do I?

Gordon You've got to remember his affliction. He can never be more than two minutes from a toilet, Sylvia.
Sylvia Affliction — it's a prostate, Gordon. Other men get it seen to. It's you. You just can't admit he has you under his thumb. You're a man now, Gordon — stand up to him.
Gordon He thinks you're just after my money. He thinks every girl's just after my money.
Sylvia Every girl? How many girls are there?
Gordon None. You know what I mean.
Sylvia And what money? He sees to it that you never have any money. I always pay for myself at the pictures and we have a season ticket at the dance hall — and we won that in a raffle!
Gordon Yes, but one day I'm going to be well off, aren't I?
Sylvia You can't live on promises for ever, Gordon. By the time he's dead his business might have gone bust. A deckchair's not the sort of thing you want every five minutes, is it?
Gordon He doesn't just sell one at a time, Sylvia. He sells hundreds. You heard him — today he was in Skegness.
Sylvia And did Skegness buy any?
Gordon No. Not this time. They had a very bad summer.
Sylvia There you are then. At least with a gas oven you can cook with it; you can only sit on a deckchair, Gordon!
Gordon Why are we rowing? I don't like us rowing.
Sylvia Then do something about it. You asked me to marry you tonight and I thought you meant it.
Gordon I did.
Sylvia So what now? We have to wait till the sun shines in Skegness do we? It's no way to live, Gordon. We might be waiting forever!
Gordon You know I like a quiet life, you know I can't stand rowing.
Sylvia Then *do* something. Don't just sit there being marred. People are saying you're a mummy's boy, Gordon.
Gordon (*horrified*) They're not!
Sylvia I'm sorry, but I have to be cruel to be kind, Gordon. I didn't want to have to tell you this but I think I must: my friend Yvonne in accounts thinks you're a bit of a wimp, a bit of a girl's blouse.
Gordon She doesn't.
Sylvia I defended you, of course, what else would I do? "You should see his body", I said, "when he's in that swimming pool", I said.
Gordon That's made me really angry, Sylv.
Sylvia Well, I'm sorry, Gordon, but truth will out. And if we're to get married you've got to change. You'll have responsibilities: a house to run, a lawn to mow, and one day, Gordon, who knows? — you might even be a father.
Gordon (*rising, determined, getting more water from the tap*) Right, that's it; nobody's calling me a girl's blouse — 'specially not that Yvonne! (*He gulps down more water*) Sod my dad, sod all of 'em, Sylvia — I'm going

Act I, Scene 2   21

through with this and I'm going to do it properly. (*He goes down on one knee*) Sylvia Lomax — will you marry me?
Sylvia (*overwhelmed but so proud of him*) Oh, yes, Gordon, I will marry you.

The Lights come up on the living-room again

Stanley enters from the hall

Stanley That lavatory's a liability. You have to wait half an hour for it to flush. I couldn't live like this, Myrtle.
Vic (*waking up again*) Is it tea time? My God, are they still here?
Myrtle Stanley, Mrs Lomax and I have been talking.
Stanley There's nothing more to be said, Myrtle; the episode is closed, over, done with. We shan't be visiting this house again. (*To Vic*) Isn't it time you got off your arse and mended that toilet?
Vic (*rising*) Here — now — just you watch it!
Stanley (*unbuttoning his coat for a fight*) Don't start threatening me, mate, or I'll knock you into the middle of next week!
Joyce Vic, please don't show us up in front of Mr and Mrs Broadbent!
Myrtle Stanley — remember your condition, please!

They ad-lib more argument

Gordon comes running in, dragging Sylvia by the hand

Gordon (*above the shouting*) Dad. Mum. I have something to say — and I want no arguments. Me and Sylvia — that is Sylvia and I — we're getting married next Easter Saturday whether you like it or not! Right?

Joyce and Myrtle smile at each other. Stanley looks aghast

Vic (*throwing his arms in the air*) God help us!

Music fills the auditorium. All the Lights fade and the actors clear the stage

SCENE 2

A month later. Saturday morning

Almost immediately, the Lights come up brightly and the music fades

Yvonne is standing on a stool being fitted with an unfinished bridesmaid's dress which at the moment is too long with bits missing. Yvonne is eating a packet of crisps and showing no interest in the dress. Myrtle is on her hands and knees with a tape measure and a mouth full of pins, etc.. Her handbag is nearby

From upstairs we can hear knocking — the sound of plumbing work in the bathroom

Myrtle Does it feel comfortable, Yvonne?
Yvonne Well, it feels comfortable, Mrs Broadbent, but it looks a bit lop-sided from up here.
Myrtle I'm a very experienced needlewoman, Yvonne; I do not make my dresses lop-sided, dear.
Yvonne I'm not criticizing, honest. It's just that my left breast seems more exposed than my right, if you see what I mean.
Myrtle That's only because it isn't finished. And you will be wearing a strapless bra remember.
Yvonne OK. I'll stop complaining. I suppose we must just say it's a miracle this wedding's taking place after what Sylvia told me about your husband. Round here, screaming and bawling she said.
Myrtle That was four weeks ago. A lot can happen in a month, Yvonne. You've just got to let Mr Broadbent think that everything's his idea and he's fine. (*She stands*) Now, how's that?
Yvonne Fine. I suppose. Actually, if you don't mind me saying so, it's the colour I'm not altogether struck on. What's it supposed to be?
Myrtle Stanley says it's Peach and Apricot Crush.
Yvonne I see. Fancy.
Myrtle And I'm going to do lemon piping round the cleavage so that should set it off nicely.
Yvonne I hope Sylvia's seen it. I wouldn't want to put her dress in the shade.
Myrtle Sylvia's dress is beautiful — nothing could put that in the shade, Yvonne.
Yvonne Where did Mr Broadbent actually find this material. On the market?
Myrtle (*laughing*) On the market! Oh, you are funny, Yvonne. No, Stanley has very close connections in the rag trade.
Yvonne I thought he made deckchairs.
Myrtle So? What do you think they're made of? Stanley's old school, Yvonne: he doesn't use plastic. (*She moves up inside the dress*)
Yvonne I'm sure red and white canvas stripes would have been better than this.
Myrtle Sorry?
Yvonne It just looks a bit "end of range" to me.
Myrtle No, Stanley's been quite good really. Of course he wouldn't hear of a registry office do. A church or nothing at all — so he had a word with the vicar and that was that. How's Sylvia coping? Getting quite nervous I expect.
Yvonne You know Sylv, Mrs Broadbent — she takes most things in her stride.

Act I, Scene 2   23

There is loud knocking upstairs

Yvonne (*looking up*) He'll have the ceiling down next.
Myrtle I know she doesn't show it but I'm sure she's excited.
Yvonne Between you and I, Mrs Broadbent, I don't think Sylvia wanted all this fuss. She'd imagined a quiet wedding.
Myrtle Simple you mean?
Yvonne Cheap I think would be a better word. She's never been extravagant has Sylvia. And Mr and Mrs Lomax aren't well off or anything.
Myrtle I am running on a very tight budget, Yvonne.
Yvonne (*looking at the dress*) Yes. I'd noticed that.
Myrtle But you can't cut corners with a wedding. (*She stands*) There now, how's that?
Yvonne What's this scrunched bit round the waist for?
Myrtle It's the semi-crinoline look. It's all the rage now for matrimonial wear.
Yvonne I shall look bigger than Sylvia. Is that the idea?
Myrtle Now could you just give me a twirl?
Yvonne Not up here, eh? I could come a cropper. Give us a hand.

Myrtle helps Yvonne off the stool. Yvonne twirls

Myrtle Yes, I can just see what it's going to be.
Yvonne Bit like "Come Dancing" really, except you'd have a job on, dancing in this.

Stanley, dressed in overalls over his suit and tie, enters from the hall. He is carrying a bucket which contains a rusty old ball cock, and a tool chest

Stanley Well, that'll be a nice surprise for them. I've fixed the toilet, Myrtle.
Myrtle What do you think, Stanley?
Stanley It's fine. At least you won't have to wait half an hour for it to flush.
Myrtle I meant the dress. Doesn't she look a picture?
Stanley Is it finished?
Myrtle Is it finished? Can you hear this, Yvonne? Men! Of course it isn't finished. I've all this to do yet.
Stanley Exquisite material, I will say that. And I got it cost.
Yvonne I can imagine.
Stanley (*giving Myrtle the bucket and the tool chest*) Get rid of these for me, would you, love? Bucket under their sink, tools in the outside shed.
Myrtle (*loaded up*) I should take it off now, Yvonne. Stanley won't look, will you, Stanley? (*During the following, she does as instructed but keeps hold of the ball cock*)

Stanley She's a good woman, my wife. Heart of pure gold, really. Sylvia's a very lucky young woman.

Yvonne attempts to free herself from the dress. Stanley watches as she strips down to her underwear, getting his eyeful of her legs etc.

Yvonne I'm glad you think so.
Stanley No doubt about it. The Lomaxes are a very ordinary family to say the least. Not at all the sort of folk we usually mix with.
Yvonne Pity. (*Caught up with the pins*) God alone knows what she's done here ...
Stanley But, "love knows no barriers", as my wife is forever saying. It's her who persuaded me to consent to this marriage. "You married me, Stanley," she said. Myrtle, you see, is also of somewhat lowly birth.
Yvonne She's been telling me she used to be a barmaid at the *Cock and Trumpet*.
Stanley Well, she did work in a back-street public house — yes. Until I rescued her. (*Eager to get his hands on Yvonne; offering to help*) May I ...?
Yvonne Here, you shouldn't be looking, Mr Broadbent!
Stanley Sorry? Oh, I do beg your pardon — I'm quite without shame, aren't I? (*He turns away and starts to remove his overalls*) All I said was "Well, if there's to be a wedding it's got to be a proper wedding — none of this back-door stuff in a registry office with a plate of pie and chips afterwards." I said, "I don't want my neighbours or my customers thinking the worst!" I said.
Yvonne I think I need a hand here.

Stanley shuffles over to assist Yvonne, his overalls round his ankles

Stanley Don't panic, Yvonne. I've done this countless times for Myrtle so I'm not embarrassed.
Yvonne I am. Try not to tug too hard, Mr Broadbent.

Myrtle appears at the living-room door with the old ball cock

Myrtle What shall I do with this, Stanley?
Stanley (*trying to free the dress*) Sorry, dear?
Myrtle This ball cock. Where do you want it?
Stanley Put it in the dustbin, Myrtle. Use a bit of common.
Myrtle (*seeing the fuss*) Is everything all right?
Stanley (*giving the dress a final tug; the material rips*) It is now, Myrtle, it is now, dear.
Myrtle Hang the dress up, Yvonne: don't leave it all higgledy-piggledy, will you?

Act I, Scene 2   25

During the following, Myrtle goes back to the kitchen and exits by the back door, moving out of sight

As Myrtle goes, Joyce arrives in the street. She is returning from shopping, carrying several plastic bags and pulling a shopping basket on wheels. She opens the front door with her key and goes into the hall

Stanley It's a good job I've got an understanding wife, Yvonne. She could have taken offence there.
Yvonne *(putting on her sweater, etc.)* I expect she's used to you by now. I've had my fill of men and their sexual antics, I can tell you.
Stanley Married yourself then, are you? *(He steps out of his overalls)*
Yvonne Have been. Twice as a matter of fact. Never again. That's what I've been trying to tell Sylvia ... but will she listen?
Joyce *(from the hall)* Coo-ee — it's only me.*(She heads towards the living-room)*

Yvonne bends down to pick up her skirt

Joyce appears at the living-room door with all her bags

Having a nice time are we? *(She sees the dress in a heap on the floor)* Lovely dress, Yvonne.
Yvonne Oh, hallo, Mrs Lomax. Yes, I've been having a fitting.
Joyce *(coming into the room)* Yes, isn't Mrs Broadbent clever? I'd be lost I can tell you. *(She sees the bird cage is still covered)* Oh, my God!
Yvonne *(startled)* What?

During the following Yvonne gets down on the floor and tries to sort out the dress in order to hang it up

Joyce Hoppy! He's still covered up. He'll be so confused — he won't know whether it's night or morning. *(She uncovers the cage)* Poor, poor Hoppy. Mummy's a bad person, isn't she?
Stanley Have I got a surprise for you, Mrs Lomax.
Joyce For me, Mr Broadbent? I don't believe you.
Stanley The next time you go to your lavatory, you'll notice the difference.
Joyce *(puzzled)* Our toilet? A surprise in our toilet?
Stanley Just wait and see — I'm not telling you — but you'll get the shock of your life.
Joyce *(delighted)* I'll bet I know what it is.
Stanley Ha, ha, just you wait and see!
Joyce You are awful, Mr Broadbent. But I was saying to Vic in bed last night: you and Mrs Broadbent have brought sunshine into our lives — haven't they, Yvonne?

Yvonne If you say so, Mrs Lomax. I'd prefer it raining myself.
Joyce (*going to the hall again, collecting her bags*) Now, I thought I'd do a nice salmon salad for our lunch: what do you reckon?
Stanley (*folding his overalls*) Oh, not for us, Mrs Lomax. We always go to the *Cosy Crumpet* for our Saturday lunch — saves Myrtle slaving away at that stove.
Joyce (*entering the kitchen, calling*) Nonsense, if you're good enough to do all this for us and our Sylvia, it's the least I can do. (*She sees the open back door*) Oh, God, I haven't left this back door open, have I? (*She closes and locks the back door*) If our Hoppy was to get out ...
Stanley (*to Yvonne*) Nice woman really, Mrs Lomax. Means well — good-hearted.
Yvonne (*hanging the dress from the central light fitting*) Well, I think so.

In the kitchen, Joyce starts to unload her bags and shopping trolley on to the table. There seems to be mountains of food

Stanley Known them long, have you, the Lomaxes?
Yvonne All my life really. I went to school with Sylvia. Then we started work together at the Gas Board. She was even a bridesmaid at both my weddings.
Stanley Children, have you?
Yvonne One, that's all, our Roy: he lives with his dad.
Stanley You're full of surprises: twice married, a mother, and now a bridesmaid.
Yvonne Yes, and a right pratt I'm going to look. I wouldn't do it for anybody but Sylvia I can tell you.
Stanley Her very best friend obviously.
Yvonne (*pinning bits to the dress*) I am. I hope I've always been there when she's needed me — especially when she found out about —— (*She stops herself in time*)
Stanley (*ears pricked*) Yes ... ?
Yvonne Let's just say she's a one-off is Sylvia. Quite unique. Not like anybody else I know.
Stanley Simple-minded you mean?
Yvonne (*offended*) I didn't say that!
Stanley I'm sorry — I didn't mean to imply ...
Yvonne If you mean she's unsophisticated — so what? I prefer that to some of the wine-drinking, party-going, wife-swopping pricks I mix with. There's a lot to be said for the simple life, Mr Broadbent.
Stanley Oh, yes — I agree with you. (*He indicates the room*) Her parents seem quite content with all this.
Yvonne Vic's always been a postman, Joyce a housewife. They've never expected much out of life so they've never been disappointed. There's nothing wrong with that either.

Stanley It'll be a big step up for Sylvia, marrying our Gordon.
Yvonne It'll be a big step all right: whether it's "up" or not remains to be seen.
Stanley I'll have you know our Gordon's considered in many circles to be quite a catch.
Yvonne I can't see why. He's hardly 007 is he?
Stanley I'm sorry ... ?
Yvonne And still firmly attached to Myrtle's apron strings and your deckchairs, no?
Stanley He's reserved, yes. Cautious, maybe. But he'll make Sylvia a very good husband. Once Gordon has plighted his troth, it'll stay plighted, I can tell you.
Yvonne (*scissors in hand*) It'd better, Mr Broadbent, otherwise you and that son of yours might find yourselves with your cobblers cut off — right?
Stanley (*appearing somewhat turned on by her threats*) Oh, I say — I can see you're a woman to be reckoned with. Live locally, do you?
Yvonne Number 34 — across the road.
Stanley I see. Live alone now I suppose.
Yvonne I do. And that's the way it's going to stay.
Stanley Well, if ever you need a handyman — you know where to come. (*He straightens his tie*) I'm especially handy in the bedroom. (*He laughs*) I mean decorating, of course.

Joyce heads into the living-room with a new piece of cuttlefish bone for the bird

Yvonne Mr Broadbent — why don't you just disappear up your own ——
Joyce (*entering the living-room*) Look what Mummy's got for Hoppy-Whoppy — a new piece of cuttlefish bone. (*She goes to the cage*)

Myrtle appears by the back door, visible through the frosted glass panel, and tries to get in during the following, knocking at the door, trying the handle, calling etc., but going unheard

Sylvia and Gordon come into the front garden from the street. Both are eating chips from a paper

Sylvia We'd better finish these out here, Gordon. Otherwise, we'll smell the house out.

They sit on the low brick wall in the garden

Joyce (*heading back to the kitchen, looking up at the dress*) I shouldn't leave that there, Yvonne — we don't want it to catch fire, do we?
Yvonne Don't we ... ?

Myrtle disappears

In the kitchen, Joyce starts to put her shopping into cupboards. Yvonne now hangs the dress on the bird cage

Sylvia Well, I don't know about you, Gordon, but I thought that vicar was a very nice man. (*Pause*) As vicars go that is.
Gordon (*eating chips*) Yes ...
Sylvia I mean — I've always thought vicars were very stuck-up people who went on and on about God all the time. But he didn't.
Gordon No ...
Sylvia And I must say I was very surprised by his apparel. I mean, his anorak was not unlike yours, was it? Mind you I did think his cycling shorts were a bit too ... well ... for a vicar anyway.
Gordon A bit tight, I thought.
Sylvia Yes, well, I wasn't going to say. But his heart's in the right place, Gordon.
Gordon He kept calling me Geoffrey.
Sylvia Yes, well, he must have so many people to deal with. At Nan's funeral the vicar there kept referring to her as Gladys when her actual name was Muriel. Dad wanted to kick up a stink but I quelled him.

There is a pause; they eat their chips

I wouldn't mind betting it's going to be a beautiful service, Gordon. And I like what he said about setting out on the road of life. I thought that was quite poetic. "It's an excursion that's bound to be hazardous," he said, didn't he?
Gordon "Think of it as a journey by bicycle over exceptionally rough terrain," he said to me.
Sylvia There you are — very poetic is that, Gordon.
Gordon He mentioned "other" women.
Sylvia Did he? When, Gordon?
Gordon While you were choosing the hymns. It was man-to-man stuff really.
Sylvia What did he say?
Gordon He said he was just going through a divorce himself and it was costing him a fortune.
Sylvia Never!
Gordon That's what he said, Sylv.
Sylvia Now that just goes to show they're human beings just like us. (*She pauses*) "Love Divine, All Loves Excelling", Gordon.
Gordon Pardon?

Act I, Scene 2

Sylvia That's the hymn I've chosen. I did consider "For Those In Peril On The Sea" because my uncle was a sailor and got drowned. But I thought the occasion didn't really merit it. (*Pause*) We want to be happy, don't we?
Gordon (*taking her hand*) We will be, Sylvia.

They sit holding hands

Myrtle comes round from the back of the house still carrying the ball cock

Myrtle I'm sorry, Gordon, Sylvia, but I'm locked out.
Sylvia Oh, dear. Come along, Mrs Broadbent, I'll let you in. (*She gives Gordon her chips, opens the front door and goes into the house*)
Gordon What're you doing with a ball cock, Mum?
Myrtle It's too long a story, Gordon. How was your visit to the vicar?
Gordon He was very nice — not very religious though.
Myrtle (*going into the house*) Yes, well, all that's gone out of fashion these days. Gordon.

Myrtle goes indoors, leaving the street door open, and heads for the kitchen. Gordon remains in the garden eating Sylvia's chips

Sylvia enters the living-room

Sylvia Oh, hallo, Yvonne. How was the fitting? (*She removes her coat and headscarf etc.*)
Yvonne What I put myself through for you, Sylvia.
Sylvia (*seeing the dress hanging from the bird cage*) Well, it certainly looks very elegant, doesn't it, Mr Broadbent.
Yvonne Elegant? It should make you look good anyway, Sylv.

Sylvia goes into the hall to hang her coat up. Myrtle has entered the kitchen where Joyce is still putting shopping into cupboards

Myrtle (*to Joyce*) I was knocking, Mrs Lomax: didn't you hear me?
Joyce (*busy at a cupboard*) You what, love?
Myrtle Never mind. Have you a new bin-liner? The one out there is full to overflowing.
Joyce What's that in your hand?
Myrtle A ball cock, dear. We go through these like Mars bars in our house.

Joyce hands Myrtle a new black plastic bin-liner from a drawer then continues with her work. Myrtle puts the ball cock into the bag, opens the back door again and goes out

Stanley *(to Sylvia)* How was the rehearsal, Sylvia?
Sylvia *(coming back into the living-room)* Well, it wasn't exactly a rehearsal, Mr Broadbent. It was more of a good talking to.
Stanley Full of meaningless advice was he? That's vicars all over. Now, I'd better get my engine seen to or we'll be stuck out there all day. Excuse me, Yvonne — nice to have met you.
Yvonne *(to herself, busily)* Wish I could say the same.
Stanley *(to Sylvia)* You have a good friend there, Sylvia. She looks like a Paris model in that dress. *(He moves to go into the hall, then stops)* Oh, by the way, there's a bill for your father. *(He produces a bill and puts it on the table)* A new ball cock and various bits for your lavatory. It'll do next time I see him. *(He leaves, appearing at the front door during the following)*
Yvonne *(to Sylvia when Stanley has gone)* I wouldn't like to be left alone with him for too long, Sylv.
Sylvia Ever such a nice man though, Yvonne.
Stanley *(to Gordon)* What a lovely girl that Yvonne is, Gordon. Now that's who you should be marrying — a real woman!
Gordon How much is all this costing, Dad? Only Sylvia's parents can't afford a fortune, you know.
Stanley Don't worry about it, lad. It's a wedding — a once in a lifetime event. Who wants to talk about money?
Gordon And this catering Mum's doing — you know how extravagant she can be. Tell her to keep it simple, eh? Cheese on sticks, stuff like that.
Stanley I leave all that to her, Gordon — she's the expert. Stop worrying, lad. *(He heads off into the street)* I'll be at the car if I'm needed.

Stanley exits to the street

Gordon continues eating chips

Yvonne *(to Sylvia)* You all right?
Sylvia Of course I'm all right, Yvonne. Why shouldn't I be?
Yvonne I see. You don't exactly radiate happiness, Sylv.
Sylvia I'm just worried about how much all this is going to cost. I mean, I know I'm having a second-hand wedding dress ...
Yvonne *(looking at her own dress)* And this will hardly set them back a fortune ...
Sylvia It's just that I never wanted all this fuss, Yvonne.
Yvonne Have you spoken to Gordon about it all?
Sylvia Well, sort of. I don't like to bother him really.
Yvonne He's going to be your husband, Sylv. You'll have to bother him sooner or later, love.

Act I, Scene 2

Sylvia He doesn't like rows, Yvonne. Or upsets. He's very placid, very tranquil.
Yvonne Thick you mean?
Sylvia Oh, Yvonne, I do wish you wouldn't be unkind about Gordon. You're my best friend and it does make things awkward.
Yvonne (*sitting beside Sylvia*) Look, Sylv — it's not too late to put a stop to all this, you know.
Sylvia But how? It's gone too far. The church is booked. The banns have been read, the cake ordered from Fitton's and everything.
Yvonne I don't see why you have to get married at all.
Sylvia How can you say that? It's all right for you, Yvonne — you've been married twice.
Yvonne Yes. And it was twice too many, Sylv. The first one spent more time in jail than he did with me. The second — well, I should have known when I found him in bed with his best man's wife. I couldn't bear to see you go through all that.
Sylvia Gordon's not like that, Gordon's different.
Yvonne How do you know? He's still a virgin — so you say.
Sylvia Yvonne, don't be coarse, please.
Yvonne Well, either he is or he isn't.
Sylvia He is. He told me. He's only ever loved me.
Yvonne Well, what happens once he gets a taste for it? What then? Men change. He might turn out like my two, after every woman in sight.
Sylvia (*rising*) I'm not sitting here listening to this, Yvonne. You're my best friend — you're supposed to be happy for me, helping me, advising me.
Yvonne That's exactly what I'm trying to do, Sylv. Advising you not to go through with it. Live with him for a while, find out what he's like. I mean, you've never even spent a night with him. Does he snore? Does he walk in his sleep?
Sylvia Of course he doesn't walk in his sleep. He'd have told me.
Yvonne Men can be very secretive, Sylv. They don't tell you everything. They wait for you to find out then it's too late.
Sylvia Gordon's not like other men — not the sort of men you've known anyway. Gordon's very caring. Very loving. He's like me; no good at outward show. He loves me, Yvonne.
Yvonne Does he? Has he told you that?
Sylvia Not in so many words, no. But I can tell. And I love him.
Yvonne (*quietly, sincerely*) I know that.

Gordon screws up the chip papers and throws them into the garden, rises, and goes into the house leaving the door ajar

Yvonne I just want you to be happy, Sylvia — I don't want things to go wrong for you.

Sylvia (*smiling at her friend*) Things won't go wrong, Yvonne. I promise.

Gordon appears at the living-room door. He doesn't like Yvonne; perhaps he's afraid of her

Gordon Hallo, Yvonne ...
Yvonne Oh, hallo, Gordon. (*She rises*) I'll see you at work on Monday, Sylv. Oh no, tell a lie, I'm having Monday off to get my feet done for the wedding.
Sylvia And you want me to explain as usual.
Yvonne Well, it is your wedding. (*She goes into the hall, calling*) Bye, Mrs Lomax.
Joyce (*still busy in the kitchen*) Bye, Yvonne.

Yvonne comes out of the house, leaving the door ajar, and exits to the street

Sylvia and Gordon look at each other in silence. He sits. During the following he picks up and reads a paperback book

Myrtle comes in from the back door carrying a broom

The Lights do not *go down on the living-room: both kitchen and living-room lights remain up on these two scenes which run together unhindered by delay*

Myrtle There we are — I've had a bit of a tidy up out there, Mrs Lomax.
Joyce I thought I'd do a salmon salad for our mid-day meal.
Myrtle (*washing and drying her hands at the sink*) Oh, not for us, thanks all the same.
Joyce It's fresh salmon. (*She holds up a tin of salmon*) I've only just bought it.
Myrtle I don't think so — I need to get home and get on with that dress. And I'm still putting the finishing touches to Sylvia's. Oh, by the way — where's my bag? — I've made a list of the kind of food I shall be preparing for the reception.
Joyce (*handing the bag to Myrtle*) Here it is.

Myrtle sits at the kitchen table and produces sheets of paper etc. from her bag

Sylvia (*to Gordon, worried*) Yvonne suspects this wedding's going to cost the earth, Gordon.

Gordon, his head buried in the novel, doesn't answer

Myrtle (*laying out her papers etc.*) I only use the finest ingredients; it costs a bit more but I've always found it worth it in the end.

Act I, Scene 2   33

Joyce (*sitting at the table*) You are working hard on our Sylvia's account, Mrs Broadbent. I'm beginning to feel guilty.
Myrtle Nonsense, I love it. And how often will I get a wedding to do for? No, I shall enjoy going to town on this for Gordon's sake. Now, I've made a list of all the prices — see. (*She shows Joyce her various lists*)
Sylvia (*irritated by Gordon reading*) Did you hear what I said, Gordon ... ?
Gordon Well, if it's all too much, Dad can cough up. He's always saying he's loaded.
Sylvia With all due respect, Gordon, I'd be happier if we could pay for it; then we wouldn't be beholden, would we?
Gordon Hmmm ... ?
Sylvia You know what I mean. If your dad pays as much as one penny towards this wedding, we're done for — we'll get it rammed down our throats for ever more ...
Myrtle Do you understand those figures, Mrs Lomax?
Joyce (*not understanding them at all*) Oh, yes ... I think so. (*She stares at the list blankly*)
Gordon You know they've mentioned about us living at our house, don't you?
Sylvia No way, Gordon. We'll get our own place.
Gordon But what if we don't? Time's getting on, Sylv.
Sylvia I'm not living at your house — and that's the end of the matter.
Gordon Perhaps we could come here.
Sylvia What, in my tiny bedroom? You can't swing a cat, let alone get a double bed in there!
Gordon Perhaps we're rushing things. Perhaps we should have waited until we could afford a house.
Sylvia We'll be waiting forever, Gordon. No, all we need is a little flat. I want us to have a life of our own.
Joyce So how much do you reckon all this'll cost, Mrs Broadbent?
Myrtle Well, as you can see, I've costed everything very meticulously — and on the safe side we're talking three to four thousand I should think.
Joyce (*ashen but putting on a brave face*) Pounds?
Myrtle (*with her usual laugh*) Of course pounds. I don't mean pence, Mrs Lomax. Oh, you are funny.
Joyce (*trying to sound as if she means it*) Very reasonable, really ...
Myrtle Well, I think so. If we'd got in professionals this would be double.

Joyce looks even paler

    As you can see: one hundred guests at approx. fifteen pounds a head — that's one thousand five hundred for a start. Then you've the hire of the reception room at the *Queen's*.
Joyce (*open-mouthed*) The *Queen's Hotel*?
Gordon You know they've hired the *Queen's* do you?

Sylvia The what ... ?
Gordon The *Queen's Hotel*, Sylv. That doesn't come cheap.
Sylvia But why the *Queen's Hotel*, Gordon? We could have had the function room at the *Cock and Trumpet* for ten pounds an hour.
Gordon Dad wouldn't be seen dead in the *Cock and Trumpet*.
Sylvia How many's been invited to this wedding, Gordon?
Gordon Twenty from your side, eighty from ours.
Sylvia Eighty! Nobody in this world has eighty relations, Gordon, not even the Queen!
Gordon Not all relations, no — but when you include all Dad's business acquaintances at the golf club ...
Sylvia This is turning into a nightmare. All we wanted was a registry office, a couple of witnesses, a piece of cream sponge and a glass of sherry. Mum and Dad can't afford all this ... !
Myrtle You're not having second thoughts, are you, Mrs Lomax?
Joyce (*lying*) No. No. And it's all for Sylvia, isn't it?
Myrtle Precisely — and it's a once in a lifetime event ... (*She checks her list again*)
Sylvia We'll have to put a stop to it all, Gordon. We'll be in debt for the rest of our lives.
Gordon But how? You heard Dad, "If you're getting married, Gordon, you're getting married proper!"
Sylvia It's blackmail — that's what it is. There'll be the church to pay for, the cars, that vicar, the bells, the choir, the *Queen's*, the food, the decor, the wine ——
Gordon Champagne, Sylv. It's bound to be champagne with Dad.
Myrtle (*looking at her list*) Oh, goodness I've forgotten the champagne: Stanley's bound to insist upon that! (*She adds champagne to her list*)
Joyce (*looking ill*) I think I need a tablet ...
Myrtle And did I tell you? He's ordered special napkins in the very finest Damask with "Gordon and Sylvia" embossed in the corner. A souvenir for ever, you see.

Joyce looks at her blankly. During the following, Myrtle adds more to her lists

Sylvia I wish I was dead, Gordon — I do.
Gordon Don't say that, Sylv ...
Sylvia We should have run away. When you asked me to marry you in the chip-shop we should have absconded. I never wanted all this.
Myrtle Oh, and of course the most expensive photographer in Manchester. But it'll all be worth it, Mrs Lomax — you'll see.

Vic enters the garden from the street, dressed now in his postman's uniform. He is in a temper, shouting at anyone who cares to listen and waving a letter in the air

Act I, Scene 2   35

Vic (*shouting*) Redundant! That's what I am: flaming redundant! A lifetime of loyalty to the perishing Post Office, and for what? Sweet FA!
Sylvia What on earth's all that out there?
Myrtle Did I hear a voice raised in anger, Mrs Lomax ... ?

Joyce is deep in thought, worried, unaware of anything

Vic (*entering the house*) Didn't I tell you? Didn't I predict disaster? (*He heads for the living-room*)
Sylvia Whatever's the matter, Dad? You're upsetting Hoppy.
Vic (*entering the living-room*) That'll have to go for a start. No money now to waste on crippled budgies!
Myrtle (*entering the room*) What's going on, Gordon — what on earth's the matter?
Gordon (*unhappy about rows*) I'm going to the toilet.

Gordon exits upstairs

Vic (*waving the letter under Myrtle's nose*) That's what's the matter, woman! (*He exits to the kitchen*)
Myrtle (*to Sylvia*) What is it, Sylvia?
Vic (*entering the kitchen, to Joyce*) And who said it wouldn't happen? Who said, "Oh, it won't happen to you"? Well, it flaming-well has, Joyce!
Joyce This wedding's going to cost a fortune, Vic. I'm at my wits' ends with it all ...
Vic (*slapping the letter on the table*) No "thank you", no "kiss my arse": just "sod off — you're not wanted any more"!
Joyce Three to four thousand, Vic ... A multitude of guests — most of them strangers — a three course, sit-down meal: smoked salmon and avocado pears, lobster thermidor with king prawns, fresh strawberries flown in from God knows where, serviettes embossed with gold — and enough champagne to sink the Titanic.
Vic (*distracted*) What are you on about?
Joyce Luxury undreamed of, Vic.
Vic Are you deaf or what, woman? We couldn't afford corned beef and chips now.
Joyce Plus the Gracie Fields Suite at the *Queen's*.
Vic (*as if to an idiot*) Can you hear me? I'm out of work, idle, on the dole, redundified, woman!

Stanley enters from the street

Stanley Now, what's all this? There's folk out there stopping to gawp.
Joyce (*almost to herself*) I'd best get that kettle on.
Vic (*following Stanley into the living-room*) And you Broadbents can hop it. You're not wanted here.

Sylvia (*almost in tears*) Dad — stop all this, please.
Vic There'll be no weddings in this house from now on!

Sylvia weeps. During the following, in the kitchen, Joyce prepares the tea things, then picks up Vic's letter and reads it

Stanley (*to Myrtle*) Excuse me, Myrtle — what's all this performance about?
Vic Performance! Performance? This isn't bloody acting, mate — this is real life — actuality is this!
Stanley What's he going on about now?
Vic No more letters for me to deliver — I'm out of work, matey, redundant. I suppose you've never heard of it.
Stanley (*picking up his bill from the table*) You'd better pay me this then. I don't want to be out of pocket. (*He gives the bill to Vic*)
Vic (*reading the bill*) New ball cock and bits — what's this?

From upstairs we hear Gordon trying to flush the lavatory

Stanley I mended your toilet, though God knows why!
Vic Thirty-four pounds and ten pence. I suppose that's gold-plated too!
Stanley You can forget the ten pence.
Vic You can forget it all, mate, because you know where you can stick your ball cock and bits!
Myrtle Oh, Mr Lomax, don't go and spoil everything, not now.
Stanley Hat and coat, Myrtle — this is no place for us. The man's demented.
Joyce (*calling from the kitchen*) Tea's on its way.
Sylvia Oh, Dad, does this mean it's all off again?
Myrtle Not off?
Stanley Off, Sylvia, off!
Vic You bet it's off. Leave my house, the pair of you, and take that daft son of yours — we've never liked him anyway!
Sylvia (*shouting*) Dad! Please!
Stanley (*helping Myrtle on with her coat*) That's it, we're not staying here to be insulted. The man's beneath contempt, Myrtle.

Joyce, in the kitchen, finishes reading the letter, her eyes full of tears, her face a study in joy, shock and disbelief. She lets out a loud cry of delight

Joyce Oh, my God, my God!
Stanley Now she's at it. This is a mad-house. If you ask me our Gordon had a very lucky escape ...

Stanley pushes Myrtle out into the hall and towards the front door

Act I, Scene 2

Myrtle (*protesting*) But all the work I've done, Stanley, all the arranging ...
Stanley To hell with all that. (*He calls upstairs*) Gordon, come on — we're leaving this house forever ...
Gordon (*in distress;off*) Help ... help, I can't seem to stop it!

Stanley and Myrtle storm out into the street and disappear

Vic grabs hold of the bridesmaid dress, pulls at it, and drags the bird cage with it; it crashes to the floor

Sylvia (*in horror*) Dad, mind our Hoppy ... !

Vic rushes out into the garden dragging the dress with him

Sylvia rushes over to the fallen bird cage and kneels

Joyce comes rushing in from the kitchen holding the letter aloft

Vic (*in the garden, shouting*) And you can take this load of old tat with you ... ! (*He flings the dress out into the street*)
Joyce (*overwhelmed*) Sylvia, Gordon, all our troubles are over — we're saved ... !

Gordon rushes down the stairs in panic

Gordon Quick, quick — I need a bucket, Mrs Lomax! I can't stop your lavatory from flushing! There's water everywhere. (*He ends up in the kitchen, searching under the sink for a bucket*)
Joyce Look, Sylv ... your father's redundancy money — five and a half thousand pounds — see ... !
Gordon (*calling, searching*) I'm sorry but you need a plumber, Mrs Lomax!
Joyce (*waving the letter*) Is nobody interested in what I'm saying? We're well off, for the first time in our lives: the wedding can go ahead, Sylvia ...!
Sylvia I'm afraid our Hoppy's dead, Mum — look. (*She holds up the dead Hoppy*)

Out in the garden, Vic sinks down on to the garden wall, head in hands

The Lights slowly fade to Black-out

CURTAIN

ACT II

Scene 1

A week later

The Curtain *rises on darkness*

A pool of light comes up first on the bird cage, still in its corner but now covered in a black cloth

A second pool of light comes up on Sylvia's white wedding dress which is neatly laid out over Vic's armchair in front of the television

Next, the street lamp rises to shed its light over the garden where Sylvia is sitting on the wall looking dejected, a hanky in her hand

The Lights now come up on the living-room where Joyce and Myrtle are sitting in silence, looking downcast. On the floor and on various tables are wedding presents wrapped in gaily coloured paper and tied with ribbons. A new gas stove stands in the room, unconnected as yet and with a huge red ribbon and a card tied around it

Silence. After a while, Joyce rises as if in a trance and looks aimlessly about the room. She sees the empty bird cage, shrouded in its black cloth, and her hand flies to her mouth to stifle a sob

Myrtle Try not to look at it, Mrs Lomax.
Joyce It's just ... on top of everything else ...
Myrtle I know, I know. But time heals. So they say. If you take my advice you'll get rid of it altogether.
Joyce But how could I, Mrs Broadbent? I'd rather have the memories than an empty space. And what if we get another bird: where would it live?

Silence. Sylvia wipes her nose and sighs deeply

The telephone rings loudly. Joyce and Myrtle look at it anxiously. Sylvia's ears prick up

Act II, Scene 1 39

Joyce (*calling loudly*) Sylvia — the telephone, love.
Sylvia (*calling*) I shan't answer it, Mum. Let it ring.
Joyce (*to Myrtle*) Who will it be, Mrs Broadbent?
Myrtle Shall I ... ?
Joyce Oh, please — it could be a tragedy.
Myrtle (*taking a deep breath, then answering the phone*) The Lomax residence; can I help you? ... I'm sorry? ... Are you sure you've dialled the correct number? (*To Joyce*) It's a man with a bad chest, Mrs Lomax — he says you've won a set of see-through night attire.
Joyce That makes a change; last time it was Paris underwear.
Myrtle Are you entered in a raffle?
Joyce Ignore it. Put the phone down, Mrs Broadbent. The man's not right in his head; he's always ringing.
Myrtle (*into the phone*) Not today, thank you. (*Shocked*) I beg your pardon ... ? (*She reacts; he has obviously rung off*)
Joyce What did he say?
Myrtle (*replacing the phone*) I must have misheard.

Silence again. Myrtle sits again. Joyce looks sadly at the card attached to the new gas stove

Sylvia comes in from the garden leaving the front door ajar

Joyce (*reading the card*) "To Sylvia and Gordon: when the honeymoon's over, get cooking! With all our love — your friends at the Gas Board"...
Sylvia (*appearing at the living-room door*) Who was it? Was it Gordon?
Myrtle No, dear. Wrong number.
Sylvia (*about the gas stove*) That'll have to go back, Mum. And all the other presents.
Joyce (*tearfully*) Oh, Sylvia, we mustn't be hasty, must we, Mrs Broadbent?
Myrtle Why not try your dress on, Sylvia. Just in case. You never know.

Sylvia doesn't answer; she goes quietly into the kitchen

The Lights come up on the kitchen

Sylvia sits at the table staring out into space

Joyce She'll have a breakdown, Mrs Broadbent; nervous seizure, that's what I dread.
Myrtle It's all Stanley's fault, Mrs Lomax. And mine. We were far too impetuous.

Joyce No, no. We're all to blame. Victor can be very hot-headed. It was losing his job that tipped the scales. He didn't really mean to upset everybody. (*With her hand to her mouth*) Or kill poor Hoppy. (*She sits*)
Myrtle Stanley was just as bad. He flares up and forgets what he's saying. It's all a storm in a teacup and meanwhile we're ruining that poor girl's life.
Joyce Doesn't Gordon realize what he's putting our Sylvia through? Doesn't he care?
Myrtle Who can tell? He hasn't spoken a word all week. Just stays locked away in his room. Won't even touch his food. Stanley's apologized. I've apologized. We've pleaded and cajoled but all he says is if this is what getting married does to people, he'd rather go into a monastery.
Joyce Sylvia's said the same. She's thinking of giving up the Gas Board and becoming a nun.

Yvonne enters from the garden dressed in a bathrobe, hair curlers and slippers

Yvonne How is she?
Joyce Oh, hallo, Yvonne. Just the same — very zombified.
Yvonne Has anybody done anything? I mean, this wedding's supposed to be tomorrow: is it on or off?
Myrtle We just don't know, Yvonne. We're praying for a miracle here.
Yvonne Has anybody cancelled the guests, rung the vicar and told him not to expect us?
Joyce How can we? What if Gordon and Sylvia change their minds? We'll look foolish turning up at an empty church.
Yvonne And what about the hotel?
Myrtle They're still expecting us. And there's all that food in my chest-freezer — the lobsters on ice — the strawberries on the aeroplane. It'll all have to be paid for.
Joyce Poor Vic. He'll have worked all his life for nothing.
Yvonne Well, if you ask me you all need your bloody heads knocked together.
Myrtle Yvonne — really! It's not our fault.
Yvonne Whose fault is it then, Myrtle? If you hadn't started all this — you and that mad husband of yours.
Myrtle (*tearful*) You see, even Yvonne blames us.
Yvonne You should have left them alone, Myrtle.
Joyce Now, stop that, Yvonne. What about you? You never wanted our Sylvia to get married in the first place.
Yvonne That's when she was getting married; now it looks as if she isn't, it's different. I can see it's what Sylvia wants — what she needs. What else has the poor cow got in life?

Act II, Scene 1   41

Joyce There's no need for that sort of talk, Yvonne. Sylvia's led a very fulfilled life until all this.
Yvonne Look, where is she? I'm going to talk some sense into her if it's the last thing I do.
Joyce She's in the kitchen. Try and get her to eat something. (*To Myrtle*) The weight's simply falling off her.

Yvonne enters the kitchen

The Lights fade in the living-room

Yvonne (*trying to be cheerful*) Hiya, Sylv. (*She sits at the table*) Excuse the way I look. I've just had a bath and washed my hair. Ready for tomorrow.
Sylvia There won't be a tomorrow, Yvonne. Or the day after that. My life is over.
Yvonne (*after an awkward pause*) I see the gas stove arrived. (*She pauses*) We all clubbed together.
Sylvia Yes, and if it was connected I'd put my head in and do away with myself.
Yvonne (*taking her hand*) Oh, come on, love. Things are not too bad.
Sylvia How can you say that, Yvonne — my life is in tatters. It's all I've ever wanted in life. To marry Gordon.
Yvonne Well, I'm sure you will ... eventually.
Sylvia Talk sense. He's deserted me. Walked out. It's been a week and he hasn't called to see me. He hasn't even rung.
Yvonne Maybe he's bracing himself, Sylv. Giving himself time to think things over.
Sylvia He's cutting it a bit fine: we're due at the altar in a few hours. A vicar will be waiting, a choir warming up ... Aunty Jessie all the way over from Mablethorpe. Why should this happen to me, Yvonne? What have I ever done to deserve all this?
Yvonne I know, love, I know ...
Sylvia I knew this was going to happen, I knew it. Me and Gordon, we've always been all right on our own — left to our own devices. We should never have let the Broadbents interfere. And look what it's costing — and all paid for with Dad's redundancy money.
Yvonne Where is your dad?
Sylvia The Post Office are giving him a party to celebrate losing his job. You see: it's almost laughable.
Yvonne (*trying hard not to laugh*) Yes, it is really.
Sylvia It's not funny, Yvonne. Even Mum's changed. She's becoming more like the Broadbents every day.
Yvonne She's excited, that's all. She wants to see you happy.

Sylvia Happy? Nobody's asked me anything, Yvonne. Nobody's even thought about the future. If we ever do get married, where are we going to live for a start?
Yvonne I assumed you'd live at the Broadbents for a while.
Sylvia Yes, that's what they assume, that's what Mum and Dad assume — everybody assumes, Yvonne. Well, I refuse to live with them. Can you imagine a life with Stanley and Myrtle Broadbent?
Yvonne Come to think of it, no, I can't.
Sylvia Well, I can. It would be pure hell. They'd probably have me making deckchairs in no time.
Yvonne (*beginning to admire Sylvia*) I've never seen you like this, Sylv. You're suddenly quite grown up.
Sylvia I am grown up. I'm a woman, Yvonne. And I'm just about to lose the only thing in life I've ever wanted. And who cares?
Yvonne I care. That's why I'm here. I want to help you sort it out.
Sylvia How, Yvonne. Tell me how!
Yvonne Well, I can provide you with a home for a start.
Sylvia What do you mean?
Yvonne I've just thought about it. You can come and live with me, Sylv.
Sylvia You?
Yvonne Why not. I'm all alone in that house. We get on. I could learn to live with Gordon — just. What do you think?
Sylvia Oh, Yvonne, it would be the answer to all my prayers.
Yvonne I could move into the single bedroom, you and Gordon could have the double: what could be simpler?
Sylvia You'd do that? For me?
Yvonne We're friends, Sylv. What are friends for?
Sylvia I can't believe it.
Yvonne But don't get too carried away, love. Where's Gordon?
Sylvia (*her face falling*) Yes, Yvonne. Where is he? Will he ever come back ... ?

The Lights slowly cross-fade from the kitchen to the living-room

Stanley comes into the garden, sees the front door still ajar, enters the house and comes into the living-room

Myrtle Oh, Stanley — any news?
Stanley No news.
Myrtle Where's Gordon now?
Stanley He went off to football practice at half-past six.
Myrtle Football practice!
Stanley Now he'll be at his stag night at the *Cock and Trumpet*.

Act II, Scene 1   43

Myrtle Stag night, Stanley!
Stanley Said it was all arranged. Wasn't going to cancel. Said he was going to get blind roaring drunk.
Myrtle Oh, my God. Can this be our son, Stanley? He never gets drunk, Mrs Lomax.
Stanley You've spoilt him, Myrtle. All this is your doing. You cosseted him when what he needed was a backhander now and again.
Myrtle So I'm to blame now am I? Me, Mrs Lomax. Did you hear him? I'm to blame!
Stanley Don't get hysterical, Myrtle. We can live without that. It's me who'll have to bear the brunt and the shame of all this. My business is going to suffer: mark my words.
Joyce Poor Mr Broadbent. Who'd have thought things would turn out like this? I think I blame our Sylvia — I do.
Myrtle Oh, don't say that, Mrs Lomax.
Joyce Yes, but she rushed your Gordon and I know your Gordon's type: they don't like to be rushed.
Stanley Mrs Lomax is right, Myrtle. Sylvia's always been a bit too fast for my liking. Anyway, it's all history now.
Myrtle Don't say that, Stanley.
Stanley Get your hat and coat, Myrtle, I've come to take you home. It's well past ten.
Myrtle How can I go home, Stanley? We need to know what's happening tomorrow.
Stanley The same as every Saturday, Myrtle. Breakfast at nine, down to Sainsbury's, lunch at the *Cosy Crumpet*, an hour in the garden, clean out Gordon's fish tank, supper and a spot of telly in the evening. Life's got to go on.
Myrtle But who'll inform the *Queen's Hotel*? Cancel all the guests? And what about those mountains of food?
Stanley It's all got to be paid for, Mrs Lomax. That husband of yours can't be allowed to get away with this — oh, goodness me, no!
Joyce Oh, I'm sure he'll not begrudge it. Vic can be very generous when he's a mind.
Stanley You could have fooled me. He still owes me for that toilet. Still, it's all water under the bridge now. I doubt we'll be meeting again. It's been an unfortunate episode in our lives. Myrtle — the car, please.

Myrtle rises to get her coat from the hall

Vic enters

Myrtle Oh, hallo, Mr Lomax — we were just about to leave.

Vic Good. (*He goes to his chair where the wedding dress is on display*) And you can take this with you.
Joyce Vic, I hope you're not drunk.
Vic I am not drunk. Shift this frock before I set light to it.
Myrtle (*rushing to rescue the dress, afraid of Vic*) We're not sure what we should do with it, Mr Lomax.
Stanley Don't encourage him, Myrtle, please.
Joyce Did you have a nice do, Vic? Were there speeches? Did they cry?
Vic Only a few of my mates turned up. Not a bloody sign of the bosses, Joyce.
Joyce Oh, dear. (*To Stanley*) Sad really, you know.
Vic A lifetime in one job, eh? I mean, I didn't expect the Postmaster General but my boss could have turned up, couldn't he, Joyce?
Stanley Shows how popular you must have been ...
Myrtle Stanley — that's enough!
Joyce I'll get that kettle on in a minute. Put your feet up, Vic. Put the telly on if you like.
Myrtle We're very worried the wedding won't take place, Mr Lomax, aren't we, Stan?
Stanley Wedding or no wedding, everything will have to be paid for. Someone will have to foot the bill.
Vic Ay, and it won't be me I can tell you.
Stanley Well, it certainly won't be me, Lomax. I shall haul you through every court in the land to get that money out of you.
Vic Do what you like. You can announce it on television for all I care: my redundancy money stays where it is, in the bank!
Joyce Now, Vic, don't be spiteful!
Myrtle We're very worried about the effect all this is having on our Gordon, Mr Lomax.
Vic Are you? I'm not. From the way your Gordon's behaving in the tap-room at the *Cock and Trumpet*, I'd have thought our Sylvia was better off out of it.
Myrtle Gordon!
Stanley Our Gordon?
Joyce Have you seen Gordon?
Vic Seen him. I should think I've seen him. You couldn't miss him. Making an exhibition of himself.
Myrtle (*pale, hand to mouth*) Oh, Stanley — my stomach's turned over.
Stanley Just say what you mean, Lomax.
Vic Standing on a table, pissed as a fart, dressed only in his football shorts and showing his arse to all and sundry.
Myrtle Our Gordon!
Stanley If you're making this up just to upset my wife ——

Act II, Scene 1   45

Vic Go and see for yourself. Mind you, you'd have to hurry: they were just chucking him out as I left. His mates seemed to be enjoying it anyway. And he was singing.
Stanley Singing. Our Gordon never sings.
Vic (*amused by it all*) You should have heard him. (*He sings*) "I'm not getting married in the morning!" (*He laughs*)
Joyce Lovely song, though.

Sylvia comes running in from the kitchen

Sylvia What is it? What's going on?
Joyce Go away, Sylvia, it'll only upset you.
Sylvia Tell me. I must know. Has Gordon been taken away?
Vic Not yet, love. But it won't be long. Any tea, Joyce?
Sylvia Please, somebody, tell me what's happened.
Stanley You've driven our son to drink, Madam. I hope you're satisfied!

Yvonne enters the living-room

Yvonne Look, isn't it time you lot went home? She's upset enough as it is.

Gordon appears in the garden. He is very drunk and is wearing only his football shorts, socks and boots — his football shirt is over his shoulders

Gordon (*a cry like an animal*) Sylvia! Sylvia ... !
Myrtle Oh, my God — he's here. Stanley, do something!
Gordon (*weeping, calling*) Sylvia Lomax — come out here — now!
Sylvia (*terrified*) He sounds demented; what shall I do?
Gordon (*on his knees, almost in pain*) I want Sylvia! Sylvia — please!
Yvonne (*to Sylvia*) Come on, love — I'll deal with him. You go up to your room.
Sylvia But what if he needs me?
Joyce Please, Sylv, do as Yvonne says. The state he's in he might do you harm.
Gordon (*shouting through the letter box*) I'm coming in to get you, Sylvia Lomax — I'm coming in to carry you off ... !
Sylvia You see: he wants me.
Gordon And you can tell my dad I'm going to kill him! Nobody can stop me — I've made up my mind!
Vic (*enjoying all this*) What did I tell you? That lad's a right bloody nutter! (*He switches on the television and sits back to enjoy himself*)
Gordon I can hear you all in there. I'm going to get my revenge on you, Dad! I'm going to tell Mum just what you get up to in Skegness!

Myrtle (*calling, loudly*) You needn't bother, Gordon. I know all about it!
Stanley Myrtle! (*Embarrassed, to the others*) I've no idea what they're on about.
Gordon And you can tell him — after that I'm going to set fire to all his deckchairs!
Stanley The boy's gone mad; we'll have to get him certified.
Myrtle He's not as mad as all that, Stanley.
Gordon (*loudly, crying*) Sylvia Lomax! I want you!
Yvonne (*taking charge*) Right, we've had enough of all this: Sylvia, upstairs — now! You lot — you'd better nip out the back. Leave Gordon to me.
Sylvia But, Yvonne ...
Yvonne (*firmly in command*) Sylvia, just shut it and do as I tell you. You lot, shift — now!
Gordon (*still shouting*) And if I can't see Sylvia, I'll set light to this house as well!
Stanley (*running to the kitchen*) Come along, Myrtle. I think he means it ...
Myrtle (*clutching the wedding dress*) I'd better take this, he could try and hack it to pieces ... (*She runs to the kitchen*)

Stanley and Myrtle exit by the back door

Joyce Vic, turn that telly off and come and take cover — now!
Vic (*laughing*) It'll take more than Gordon Broadbent to shift me from here.
Gordon (*through the letter box*) Is Mr Lomax in there too? 'Cos I'm going to kill him as well ...
Vic (*quickly changing his mind, turning off the television*) I think I'd best come with you, Joyce ... just in case ...

Vic and Joyce exit hurriedly through the kitchen and out the back door, slamming it shut behind them

Sylvia What if he's got a weapon, Yvonne? Concealed about his person.
Yvonne Sylvia, you're talking cobblers, love. Now go upstairs and wait there.

Yvonne pushes Sylvia into the hall

Sylvia (*being pushed by Yvonne into the hall*) But what if he insists ...
Yvonne Leave him to me. I'm an expert at this. I've had to deal with drunken buggers all my life!
Sylvia (*heading up the stairs*) I can't think what's come over him ... I've never seen him like this before ...

Act II, Scene 1   47

She exits

Yvonne opens the front door to discover Gordon on his hands and knees

Gordon (*weeping*) Sylvia! Open this door — now! (*He looks up and sees Yvonne standing there*) Oh. It's you, is it? I want a word with you ...

During the following, Yvonne helps the near legless Gordon to his feet, guides him into the house, along the passage and into the living-room

Yvonne Come on, sunshine: up you get before the neighbours send for the police ...
Gordon (*his speech slurred by drink*) I don't like you, Yvonne ... I don't like you at all ...
Yvonne No, well, I'm not exactly in love with you, Gordon — but that's life ...
Gordon It has come to my notice that you, Yvonne, have been defaming my good name ...
Yvonne Oh, yes? Well, after this performance tonight that shouldn't be too difficult ...
Gordon You've been putting it about that I'm a bit of a mummy's boy ... unmanly ... a bit of a girl's blouse ...
Yvonne Why, is that not so then?

Gordon nearly falls

Careful.
Gordon I was just about to set fire to this house I'll have you know ... but I haven't any matches ... (*During the following, he searches in his pocket for matches*)

Yvonne sits Gordon in Vic's chair

Yvonne There we are — safe and sound. Now, you hang on there ... strong black coffee is what you need ... (*She goes into the kitchen, switches on the kettle which has part boiled, and puts coffee into a mug*)
Gordon (*dazed*) Well, I'd like you to know: from this day forward I'm quite capable of standing on my own two feet ... ! (*He slides off the chair and on to the floor*) Things have happened this week which have opened my eyes, Yvonne. (*He is still searching his pockets for matches*) Where's Sylvia? I want Sylvia ...
Yvonne (*calling from the kitchen*) She's not here, Gordon. (*She makes him a mug of black coffee during the following*)

Gordon I demand to see her ... I have things to say to her ...
Yvonne She's gone.
Gordon Gone. Gone where?
Yvonne Out of harm's way. You've treated her very badly since last Saturday.
Gordon I've treated her badly: what about me? It's been the longest — longest week of my life ...
Yvonne (*returning to him with the mug of coffee*) Here, get this down you. My word, Sylvia was right: you have got a good body, haven't you? Great legs, Gordon.
Gordon (*half asleep now*) What ... ?
Yvonne (*sitting beside him on the floor*) Never mind. Come on — drink this.

Yvonne helps Gordon to drink

Why are you half-naked?
Gordon I've been dancing ... and singing ... I've been celebrating. (*He dribbles coffee*)
Yvonne (*wiping Gordon's mouth as if he were a baby*) I wouldn't have thought there was a great deal to celebrate.
Gordon (*attempting to drink again*) What is this?
Yvonne Don't worry — it's only coffee. How much stuff have you put back tonight, Gordon?
Gordon (*counting on his fingers*) I've had ... five lager and blackcurrants ... three large Bacardi and cokes ... and two Babychams ... a packet of cheese and onion crisps and ... (*he hiccups*) some nuts.
Yvonne And stripping off by the looks of it.
Gordon (*a hand on Yvonne's legs*) You've got nice legs too, Yvonne.
Yvonne (*rising and moving away*) All right — that's quite enough of that.
Gordon And you're half undressed as well. Were you just going to bed?
Yvonne Look, Gordon — you and I have to do some very serious talking. Do you intend to marry Sylvia in the morning or not?
Gordon (*sobering up slightly*) How can I? They won't leave us alone.
Yvonne Who won't leave you alone, Gordon?
Gordon My lot. My parents. Stanley and Myrtle. They want to stage manage my entire life and I'm tired of it. (*He pauses, then begins to weep*) What am I going to do, Yvonne?
Yvonne Well, it's no use crying about it. You've got to change your ways, Gordon; stand up for yourself.
Gordon I have. I've rebelled. I am never going home again. I've cut myself free of Stanley and Myrtle ... forever.
Yvonne And Sylvia by the looks of it.
Gordon Is she upset?

Act II, Scene 1   49

Yvonne What do you think? You've wounded her very deeply, Gordon.
Gordon (*getting to his feet very unsteadily*) Oh dear ... oh dear, oh dear ... I suppose she hates me now. (*Swaying, he tries to focus on the gas stove and the other presents*) Is that — that looks like a gas stove. (*He holds on to a chair at the table*)
Yvonne They're all your wedding presents: aren't people good?
Gordon They care about us? (*He sits at the table, head in hands*)
Yvonne (*sitting opposite him at the table*) Look, Gordon, listen to me. Sylvia and me, we've been talking tonight. I know all this fuss over the wedding has annoyed you. It's annoyed Sylvia too, but she was willing to go through with it for your sake.
Gordon And I was willing to do the same for her. I assumed she just wanted to please my parents.
Yvonne Oh, come on. You're marrying Sylvia because you want to. Because you love her.

Silence

Gordon (*looking across the table at Yvonne*) Do I?
Yvonne (*looking at him*) Sorry?
Gordon (*almost sober now and very serious*) I said "Do I?". I'm not sure I do, Yvonne.
Yvonne I see.
Gordon How can you be sure you love someone, Yvonne. Tell me.
Yvonne (*uneasy*) You just know, Gordon, You know inside. You feel good inside.
Gordon Well, I don't. I've never felt it. Oh, don't get me wrong, I'm happy with Sylvia, I'm content in her company; she's the only girl I've ever really known.
Yvonne But you're not in love with her?
Gordon (*quietly, head bent*) No. 'Fraid not.
Yvonne (*quietly*) I see.
Gordon Did you love both your husbands? Did you feel good inside about them?
Yvonne No. No, I don't suppose I did. But they were different, Gordon. I'm different. You and Sylvia suit each other — you belong together.
Gordon You didn't used to say that. You used not to like me.
Yvonne (*rising, moving away*) I think I'm beginning to like you even less.
Gordon Why? Because I tell the truth? Because I don't delude myself? What's all this "love" about anyway?
Yvonne Oh, come on, Gordon — it's too late at night for all this.
Gordon Does Stanley love Myrtle — or she him? I've lived with them all my life and I've never seen any signs of it. Why then should I love Sylvia?

Perhaps I don't know how to. And why should my not loving her prevent me from marrying her? She'll care for me, and I'll care for her. What more could we possibly want?

Yvonne A family perhaps. Children.

Gordon Ahh, yes. Children. That always crops up. Correct me if I'm wrong, but isn't that to do with sex — nothing to do with love at all?

Yvonne Look, Gordon, I'm confused. Either you're being very cynical or you're more naïve than I thought.

Gordon I am naïve. I admit it. I'm thirty-two and I know nothing. Is there any shame in that? I need someone to teach me.

Yvonne (*getting annoyed with him*) Sylvia will teach you.

Gordon (*mockingly*) Sylvia! She knows less than I do. (*A beat*) Did you know I've never touched her? Oh, I've held her hand in the pictures, I've pecked her on the cheek when we say good-night, but that's all. So what can Sylvia teach me?

Yvonne You'll teach each other. You'll learn about it together. It's nature, Gordon. These things happen naturally.

Gordon And what if they don't — what then? We become like Stanley and Myrtle, do we? Joyce and Vic? Like the guys at my football club who go back to their wives and say "I love you" hoping it'll smooth things over.

Yvonne You've never said that to Sylvia — she told me.

Gordon Why should I? It wouldn't be true. But she knows I'm content to be with her when I'm not playing football or swimming. Now, they do make me feel good inside, Yvonne. Is that wrong?

Yvonne I don't know. I suppose not. People do whatever makes them happy in the end.

Gordon (*after a pause*) Tell me. You're a woman of the world, twice married. What makes you feel good inside?

Yvonne Shall I tell you? Honestly? Sitting up in bed in the evening, on my own, watching telly with a big pot of tea and some hot buttered toast. Me, myself, my double bed, tea and the telly.

Gordon (*smiling at her*) Telly in the bedroom and crumbs in the bed. That's real decadence, Yvonne.

Yvonne For me, yes, Gordon. I don't need men. Making my life a misery, on at me all the time, coming home drunk, knocking me about, screwing every woman they can lay their hands on ...

They look at each other

Why did you ask Sylvia to marry you? You seemed happy with things as they were.

Gordon I was. But I'm not entirely selfish. At least I try not to be. I could see it was what Sylvia wanted. Also, you'll laugh, you had a lot to do with it.

Act II, Scene 1 51

Yvonne Me.
Gordon You'd called me a mummy's boy. That made me angry. It's the last thing in the world I am. I may be inexperienced, naïve, but I'm not a mummy's boy. I do not love Myrtle. Or my dad.

Silence. He looks down at his hands. She looks at him from behind

Yvonne I told Sylvia tonight that if you two do get married tomorrow ... you can move in with me.

There is no reply

You could have my double bed and I'll sleep in the spare room. (*A beat*) Until you find a place of your own at least.

He looks up at her. Something unspoken seems to hang in the air

It'd be a start. At least you wouldn't have to live with Stanley and Myrtle.
Gordon I wouldn't anyway. I've told you. I'm never going back.
Yvonne You'll have to go somewhere, Gordon. What about tonight? Where will you sleep?
Gordon (*after a pause, looking at her again*) At your place? (*A beat*) We could drink tea and watch the telly. I like the sound of it.
Yvonne (*dismissing him*) Don't be silly, Gordon.
Gordon We could say I was too drunk to go home. It wouldn't be safe to have me around. Please.
Yvonne And you'll marry Sylvia? You'll go through with it?
Gordon Yes. Then off on our two-day honeymoon in Fleetwood. (*A beat*) To do my stuff. (*A beat*) I like you, Yvonne. I feel I've got to know you at last. I feel ...
Yvonne You feel what, Gordon ... ?

Sylvia enters from upstairs

Sylvia (*quietly*) Hallo, Gordon.
Gordon Hallo, Sylvia.
Sylvia I'm sorry, Yvonne. I had to come and see what was happening? (*A beat*) I'm glad you came back, Gordon.
Gordon (*quietly, smiling*) So am I. You OK?
Sylvia (*simply*) I'm fine. Does this mean ... ?
Gordon (*simply*) Yes. Tomorrow. At noon.
Sylvia You don't mind all the fuss then?
Gordon Not if you don't.
Yvonne I'd best be off — leave you two to it.

Gordon I'll be across in a minute.

Sylvia looks at Gordon

I can't go home, Sylv. I couldn't face them. Yvonne's very kindly offered her spare room
Sylvia (*delighted*) Oh, you are good, Yvonne. (*To Gordon*) Has she told you about ... ?
Gordon Yes, she's told me.
Sylvia It'll make all the difference. And I know you two will get on — eventually.
Yvonne (*feeling awkward*) I'll see you in the morning, Sylv. (*She kisses Sylvia's cheek*) Sleep well.
Sylvia I shall now. You'll help me dress tomorrow?
Yvonne Course I will. Good-night — God bless.

Yvonne leaves the house, closing the front door behind her. She lingers for a moment before going off into the street

The Lights on the garden and kitchen fade, leaving only the living-room lit in a cosy night-time glow

Gordon, almost sober now, looks across at Sylvia, smiles and holds out his hand. She smiles and comes to sit beside him on the sofa, hand in hand with him

Gordon (*quietly*) What a life, eh, Sylv?
Sylvia Yes. Still, things should be different after tomorrow.
Gordon Fat chance of that, Sylv.
Sylvia Gordon!
Gordon You know what I mean. We've got to be firm, Sylvia. Stand on our own two feet. Always strong, always straight with one another.
Sylvia (*worried*) Yes.
Gordon Yvonne made me see sense tonight. She's not that bad really, I suppose.
Sylvia She's not bad at all. (*A beat*) Did she say anything?
Gordon She said a lot, one way and another.
Sylvia Anything about me?
Gordon Sort of. About you — about me. What is it? What's on your mind?
Sylvia I've had a lot of time to think this week, Gordon. I thought I'd lost you, I thought I might never see you again. And I sort of promised myself that if you did come back, and before we did get married, well, I vowed I'd always tell you the truth. (*A beat*) I'm illegitimate, Gordon.

Act II, Scene 2   53

Gordon (*putting a hand round her shoulders*) Oh, Sylv. What the 'eck does that matter? If you want the truth — I believe Myrtle and Stanley just got to the altar in time. Don't worry about it. It's nothing ...
Sylvia There's more, Gordon. (*A beat*) I'm not who you think I am. Mr and Mrs Lomax ... well, they aren't my real parents: I was adopted.
Gordon (*quietly, letting it sink in*) I see.
Sylvia It seems my real mother wasn't married and she abandoned me; she left me in a telephone box. (*Tears fill her eyes*)

Gordon, half drunk, half sober, is obviously moved by Sylvia's simplicity

Gordon, please say you don't mind, please say it won't make any difference.
Gordon You're daft, you. Did you know that? Of course I don't mind. And it makes absolutely no difference at all.
Sylvia (*smiling at Gordon*) Thank you. I feel so much better now. Everything's going to be all right, Gordon.

They settle back on the sofa, his arm still around her. As they do so ——

The Lights slowly fade to Black-out

Music fills the auditorium

A pair of ladies' shoes in a box is set in the living-room and Sylvia's Valentine card is put on display

As quickly as possible the lights come up again on:

Scene 2

The Big Day

It is the following morning. The weather looks gloomy, overcast. As the scene progresses, the Light outside the house gets steadily darker

Vic is sitting in his chair, stiff and silent; he is dressed in a hired grey morning suit and on his lap is a grey top hat. He looks decidedly uncomfortable

We hear a distant roll of thunder. Soon it will rain

After a moment, Joyce enters from upstairs. She too is dressed for the wedding in an unsuitable floral dress and bedroom slippers. She carries a huge and, for her, unsuitable hat. She goes to the mirror in the living-room

Joyce This hat won't stay on, Vic. (*She tries it on*) It makes me look like the leaning tower of Pisa — what d'you think?
Vic (*not even looking at her*) Going to piss down. That's what it's going to do, Joyce. Tipple down and catch us all out there.
Joyce I'm not used to hats, that's what it is: my head's the wrong shape for a hat. How do I look? (*The hat slides off her head*)
Vic (*without moving, like a tailor's dummy*) Can't I take this tie off a minute, Joyce?
Joyce No, Vic, you can't. It's taken all morning to get it on. (*She removes the hat*) Oh, it'll just have to wait. I should have chosen my own hat — I saw this lovely little pill-box one in paradise blue, but Myrtle said she didn't like it.
Vic Can't I watch *Football Grandstand*?
Joyce No, Vic. We've got a wedding!
Vic I don't like weddings — I never did.

Joyce sits, removes her bedroom slippers and puts on the new pair of shoes from the box

Joyce Now don't start all that.
Vic They're bad luck in our family. I'd rather have a funeral any day.
Joyce My new shoes, Vic — what d'you think?
Vic At least with a funeral you're getting rid of somebody. A wedding you're taking somebody on, aren't you?
Joyce Our Hoppy would have been proud, Vic. He'd have been chirping away in his little cage.
Vic That's right, bring that up again, spoil everything.
Joyce (*rising, inspecting her shoes*) I'm simply making an observation.
Vic Any road, once our Sylvia's gone I'm getting shut of that cage. Gives you the bloody creeps stuck there.
Joyce It's staying where it is, Vic. I shall be getting a new bird anyway. One with two legs this time. I'll need something to replace our Sylvia.
Vic Remember my sister's wedding? That was a mess too. She turned up at one church, him at another. The pair of them very nearly married somebody else.

Joyce starts to tidy away the box and its tissue paper etc.

Joyce Are you just going to sit there? There's things to be done, Vic.
Vic I can't move, can I? Not in all these nancy clothes.
Joyce I wish you'd stop saying that. It's what top people wear at weddings.
(*She busies herself moving the presents into a pile by the door*)

Vic Yes, well, we're not top people, are we? We've been too influenced by the Broadbents. Bossed about — made to feel inferior. And it's costing the earth!

Another distant roll of thunder

Joyce Oh, I hope it doesn't rain, Vic. That'll put the mockers on things.
Vic (*about the thunder*) What do you think that is, woman? Thunder is that. An omen if ever there was. She should have stayed single.

Stanley and Myrtle come from the street into the garden. They too are dressed for the wedding, she in a floral pattern and hat, he in his greys and top hat. Myrtle carries her handbag, a box of carnations and two bouquets; he is carrying Gordon's suit and top hat on a hanger

Myrtle (*ringing the doorbell*) Take the suit across, Stanley — take Gordon's suit across to Yvonne's.
Stanley She might not be up.

Joyce moves to answer the front door

Myrtle Of course she'll be up; so will Gordon, he's getting married.

Joyce opens the front door

Oh, good-morning, Mrs Lomax. I'm all butterflies here.
Stanley Why he had to stay across there beats me. He's got a home, hasn't he?
Myrtle It's what he wanted, Stanley. We can't argue with that. Now take that suit across to him.

Stanley exits to the street again with the suit and hat

Myrtle goes indoors. Joyce leaves the door ajar

Myrtle (*entering the living-room*) Now, we'll need to get all those presents down to the *Queen's*, Mrs Lomax; Stanley will take them. (*She puts the box of flowers on the table*) Good-morning, Mr Lomax, the great day's here at last. How's the blushing bride? (*She takes a carnation from the box and starts to pin it to Vic's lapel*)
Joyce She was up in the night feeling bilious; all the excitement I expect.
Myrtle Is she dressed?

Joyce She was supposed to be waiting for Yvonne to dress her, but I said, "Get on with it," I said.

Myrtle Yvonne's not been across then? Oh dear, I do hope she's not unpunctual; weddings are supposed to go like clockwork, Mrs Lomax. (*She stands back to survey the effect of Vic's buttonhole*) There we are, Mr Lomax. You do look nice — doesn't he look nice, Mrs Lomax?

Vic raises his eyes to heaven

Myrtle takes another flower and pins it to herself at the mirror

Joyce Victor thinks it'll rain before long.

Myrtle Nonsense. It'll be scorching by dinner time. "Happy the bride the sun shines upon", eh, Mr Lomax?

Joyce Is there a flower for me, Mrs Broadbent?

Myrtle All that business last night did upset Stanley and I. We thought our Gordon had become deranged with it all.

Joyce (*taking her hat and a flower with her to the kitchen*) A bacon sandwich, Mrs Broadbent? A cup of tea?

Myrtle Oh, no thanks.

Vic (*calling to Joyce*) I'll have a bacon sandwich, Joyce.

Joyce (*in the kitchen, calling back*) You're getting nothing, Victor! (*She stands before the kitchen mirror, putting on her flower and her hat, during the following*)

Myrtle You won't be wanting food, Mr Lomax. You'll spoil your appetite for the wedding feast.

Vic There's nothing there I can keep down. I've seen the menu, filth, all of it.

Myrtle Well, I will admit it's a connoisseur's banquet, Mr Lomax — but I'd hardly call it "filth".

Vic I'm paying for it. There should have been something I can eat: a bit of boiled ham, sausage rolls, a few crisps.

Myrtle (*laughing*) Oh, you are the limit, Mr Lomax. Can you hear this, Mrs Lomax?

Joyce (*at the mirror*) I've got this blemish back again. On my face. It must be something to do with nerves.

Stanley returns from across the street and enters the living-room

Stanley There's something funny going on over there, Myrtle. Yvonne, still in her night attire, just grabbed the suit and shut the door in my face.

Myrtle Is Gordon up? You know what he's like for getting out of bed.

Act II, Scene 2   57

Stanley I thought it best not to enquire. Not after last night. I've washed my hands of him.
Myrtle (*pinning a flower to Stanley*) Now don't talk like that, Stanley. Get them married; then we can sort things out.
Stanley But they're going to live at Yvonne's, Myrtle. When there's a perfectly good bedroom at home.
Myrtle If that makes them happy, why upset the apple cart? We've had enough heartache this week.
Stanley Well, if you want my opinion ——
Vic (*to himself*) We don't ...
Stanley — it's a funny way to start married life. Living with a stranger.
Myrtle (*adjusting his tie etc.*) Yvonne's a friend of the family — she's been like a sister to Sylvia. Now get all those presents into the car for me.
Stanley (*to Vic*) I notice you're sitting on your backside as usual. (*He starts picking up presents*)

Joyce enters from the kitchen, her hat and flower fixed

Joyce I'll give you a hand with those, Mr Broadbent.
Stanley (*about the gas stove*) We're not taking that I hope: I'm not risking that in the Bentley!
Joyce No, that can go across the road — that's where they'll be living. (*She collects some presents*)
Myrtle There's dozens more at the *Queen's*.

Stanley and Joyce exit into the street, carrying presents

Myrtle (*to Vic*) I was down there at seven this morning, laying on all the food, dressing the tables, instructing the waitresses, etc.. I'm quite clapped out, Mr Lomax.
Vic So am I. I'll be glad when it's all over.
Myrtle (*going to the kitchen*) Now, I'm sure Mrs Lomax must have some shoe polish somewhere. I've scuffed my shoes and I daren't turn up at a wedding in scuffed shoes — Stanley would go mental ... (*She starts fishing in drawers and cupboards looking for polish and a cloth*)

Sylvia comes downstairs in her white wedding dress and carrying her veil. She is obviously feeling good and hoping for a comment from someone

Sylvia Hallo, Dad.
Vic (*not turning to see her*) If I had to live with that woman it'd drive me mad!
Sylvia What do you think ... ?

Vic I wouldn't care but I'm paying for all this. I've worked all my life for this ...

In the kitchen, Myrtle has come across polish and a cloth. She opens the back door and heads out to polish her shoes

Myrtle (*to herself*) I'd better do this out here; Stanley says you must never polish shoes where there's food ...

Myrtle exits

Sylvia (*entering the empty kitchen to show Myrtle her dress*) Look, Mrs Broadbent ... it's a very nice fit ... when you consider it wasn't made for me ...

Joyce and Stanley come back into the living-room for the last of the presents

Joyce If only that rain will hold off, Mr Broadbent, we should have a nice day ...
Stanley May I say how attractive you're looking, Mrs Lomax.
Joyce (*as she collects presents and goes out again*) Oh, do you think so? Well, I've Mrs Broadbent to thank really: she came and chose my clothes for me ...
Stanley (*collecting the last of the presents*) My wife's always had excellent taste. And isn't it about time we dropped all this Mr and Mrs stuff? I could call you ——
Joyce Joyce ... ?
Stanley And you could call me ——
Joyce Stanley ... ?

They both laugh as they exit again into the street

Sylvia (*calling to Myrtle in the back yard*) You'd hardly notice this piece in the back, Mrs Broadbent — it's so expertly done.

Sylvia moves to the kitchen mirror and starts putting on her veil, turning so that we can see the back of the dress. Although well done, we can plainly see that a new panel has been fitted into the back of the dress

Vic (*calling to no one in particular*) How much longer have I to sit here?

Yvonne, her bridesmaid dress on but as yet not done up at the back, enters from the street doing her hair with a brush

Act II, Scene 2

Yvonne I know ... I'm late ...

Joyce returns from the car, following behind Yvonne

Joyce You're all undone at the back, Yvonne.
Yvonne (*entering the house*) I know, Mrs Lomax ... we overslept, didn't we? ... I mean I overslept!

Stanley follows Joyce on

Stanley Would you like me to do you up, Yvonne? I'm very handy that way.
Yvonne Just keep that mad sod away from me, Mrs Lomax. Where's Sylv — upstairs? (*calls*) Sylv ... ?
Sylvia (*putting on her veil at the kitchen mirror*) I'm in here, Yvonne. It's a good job I didn't wait for you ...
Yvonne (*calling to Vic*) 'Morning, Mr Lomax. Lovely day for it ... (*She heads for the kitchen*)
Vic (*to himself*) I shall be missing *Football Grandstand* for this ...
Yvonne (*entering from the kitchen*) I'm really sorry, Sylv. What with one thing and another ... (*She looks at Sylvia, genuinely moved; her eyes fill with tears*) Oh, Sylv ... !
Sylvia (*simply*) Do I look nice?

Myrtle enters from the back, polish and cloth in hand

Myrtle (*overcome*) Oh, Sylvia ... you look lovely. (*She gets her handbag*) And that reminds me ... (*She calls*) Stanley — come and look at Sylvia.
Yvonne (*kissing Sylvia on the cheek*) Sylvia, love — you really do look beautiful.
Joyce (*entering the kitchen, overwhelmed*) Oh, Sylv. I can hardly believe it. What a picture of happiness. (*She calls*) Vic, have you see your daughter?
Stanley (*entering the kitchen*) You look quite nice, Sylvia. Myrtle's done you proud.
Myrtle (*producing a blue garter and a simple cross and chain from her bag*) Here we are, Sylvia: something old, something new, something borrowed and something blue, remember. The chain's an old one of mine, your shoes are new, the dress is borrowed because I would like it back — and a nice blue garter for you.
Sylvia Thank you, Mrs Broadbent.
Joyce (*taking Sylvia's arm*) Come on, love, show your dad.

Joyce guides Sylvia though to the living-room. Myrtle follows them and puts the chain round Sylvia's neck. Stanley follows behind. Yvonne remains in the kitchen

Sylvia (*standing* C) What do you think, Dad? (*Simply*) It's all I've ever wanted really.
Vic (*rising*) You look smashing, love. And you deserve it. You've waited long enough.
Joyce Vic ... !

Only Yvonne has remained in the kitchen. She sits at the table, troubled

Myrtle Just wait till Gordon sees you in church, Sylvia: he'll fall in love with you all over again — won't he, Stanley?
Stanley (*looking at his watch*) If he's ever ready on time.
Myrtle (*looking at her own watch*) Now, if we get those presents down to the *Queen's*, make a final check on the catering then get back here ready to be taken to the church ....
Joyce (*about the stove*) Couldn't we get rid of that? We don't want to get landed with it.
Sylvia Dad, you could give Mr Broadbent a hand over the road with this.
Vic Me? With my back?
Stanley I'm not dressed for moving gas stoves ...
Myrtle Oh, Stanley, it won't kill you.
Joyce Victor, do shift yourself: just because you've lost your job doesn't mean you can sit there bone idle!
Vic (*rising*) Do this, do that: I'd be better off out of it, I would!

Vic and Stanley pick up the gas stove and carry it out into the street during the next exchange

Sylvia I'd better help Yvonne to get ready.

Sylvia, still with the garter in hand, goes into the kitchen

Myrtle Now if you come with us, Mrs Lomax, you can have a sneak preview of what I've done at the *Queen's* — after all, your husband is paying for it all.
Vic (*overhearing*) Ay, and if I don't like it, I'm not paying.
Stanley And if you refuse to pay, I shall sue, Lomax.
Myrtle Now, our car's due here at eleven thirty ...
Stanley (*calling back from the hall*) Do stop fussing, Myrtle.
Myrtle (*to Joyce*) Men! They think weddings happen by themselves!

Gordon appears from the street. He is half-dressed in his greys, braces still hanging, waistcoat and jacket over his arm, top hat on his head. He is putting on his tie

Act II, Scene 2   61

Vic and Stanley appear at the front door with the stove

Stanley You can't come in here, lad, it's not on.
Gordon How's Sylvia: is she ready?
Stanley She is ready — and looking the picture of happiness.
Gordon (*worried about something*) Is Yvonne with her?
Stanley Indeed she is. I hope you've left Yvonne's door open.
Gordon Yes. I'm sorry about last night, Mr Lomax. Too much to drink. Not used to it.
Vic That'll change once you're married, lad. (*To Stanley*) Left hand down a bit ... down a bit, you fool!
Stanley Don't call me a fool, Lomax — otherwise I'm likely to drop this thing on your foot!

Stanley and Vic disappear into the street

Gordon tries to listen at the open front door as he continues to dress

Sylvia You all right, Yvonne? You look worried.
Yvonne What? Oh, yes, Sylv. I'm fine. (*She attempts a weak smile*)
Sylvia Come on, I'll do your hair. (*She takes the brush from Yvonne and starts to do her hair*)
Myrtle Right, Mrs Lomax, if we get into the car we can wait for Stanley. (*She goes out into the hall, calling*) Shan't be long, Sylvia — Yvonne.
Joyce (*following Myrtle out*) These new shoes are killing me already. I should have broken them in, see.

Gordon hears the women coming and dodges out of sight round the side of the house

Another roll of thunder

Myrtle (*coming out of the house*) You see — what did I say? It's clearing up.
Joyce (*looking up at the sky, doubtful*) If you say so, Mrs Broadbent ...
Myrtle And isn't it time you started calling me ...
Joyce Myrtle ... ?
Myrtle Yes. And I could call you ...
Joyce Joyce ... ?

They disappear into the street laughing

Gordon, now fully dressed but nervously carrying his top hat, comes into view. He carefully watches the women go then quietly slides into the house. He stops in the hall, by the living-room door, and listens to the next exchange between Sylvia and Yvonne

Sylvia (*doing Yvonne's hair*) I thought you were getting your hair done specially, Yvonne.
Yvonne Well, I was, but I got up late, didn't I?
Sylvia How was Gordon?
Yvonne (*in a panic*) What?
Sylvia Gordon, After all that fuss last night?
Yvonne (*rising*) He's fine. I think. Look, that'll do, Sylv. It doesn't matter how I look, does it?
Sylvia Don't be silly. Of course it matters. I want you to look nice too, Yvonne.
Yvonne What — in this?
Sylvia It's fine. Come on, I'll do you up at the back. (*She starts to do up the buttons or whatever at the back of Yvonne's dress*)
Yvonne (*after a pause, something on her mind*) Sylvia?
Sylvia Did he sleep well? Was he restless?
Yvonne (*on edge*) How would I know, Sylv. How would I know that?
Sylvia All right, calm down. Anyone would think it was you getting married.
Yvonne Sylvia, listen to me. Are you sure you want me to be your bridesmaid?
Sylvia Sorry?
Yvonne Perhaps you'd rather change your mind.
Sylvia What are you on about now?
Yvonne It's not too late, love. It's never too late.
Sylvia Oh, you are silly, Yvonne. Who else would I choose? You're my best friend. Have been all my life.
Yvonne It's just that ...
Sylvia Just that what ... ?

In the hall, Gordon is looking very nervous

Yvonne I'm not sure you should be doing this, Sylv. (*She turns to look at Sylvia now*) Honestly — I don't.
Sylvia You're not still on about that, are you?
Yvonne It's such a big step, Sylv. A very big step, love. And marriage is never all it's cracked up to be.
Sylvia Ours will be. I'm not like you, Yvonne. You chose unwisely and in haste, remember? I recall telling you that — both times. (*She starts to arrange the front of Yvonne's dress*) You should have been like me and chosen Gordon. (*She laughs*) Well, you know what I mean ...

Gordon drops his hat; his hand flies to his mouth nervously

(*Calling*) Is that you, Dad ... ?

Act II, Scene 2   63

Yvonne (*in panic, knowing who it might be out there*) Finish my hair, Sylv. I'm sorry, I'm just being daft: take no notice.

Yvonne sits again. Sylvia finishes her hair. Gordon picks up his hat and creeps to the front door just in time to meet Vic who has entered from the street

Gordon (*keeping his voice down*) Oh, hallo, Mr Lomax. (*He laughs nervously*)
Vic You shouldn't be here, lad. It's unlucky.
Gordon It's all right. I wonder, Mr Lomax — would you mind awfully waiting over at Yvonne's for a while?
Vic (*puzzled*) What for?
Gordon Shhh! Keep your voice down. Yvonne's having a quiet, friendly chat with your Sylvia. It'd be a shame to disturb them, eh ... ?
Vic A chat. What about?
Gordon (*thinking on his feet*) Oh, you know — this and that — woman's talk. (*He winks knowingly*)
Vic Oh, I see. About tonight you mean. (*He winks*)
Gordon That's right. Your Sylvia's not exactly clued up about all — that. If you know what I mean.
Sylvia No. But I wouldn't have thought you knew much more.
Gordon (*looking along the hall, straightening his tie*) Oh, I do now, Mr Lomax. (*Suddenly aware of what he's said*) I mean — I had a word with my best man last night. He's like Yvonne; been married twice. So if you wouldn't mind. (*He attempts to push Vic towards the street*)
Vic But I wanted to watch the football on the telly.
Gordon You can watch it at Yvonne's. She won't mind.
Vic (*going*) Are you sure ... ?
Gordon Not a bit — make yourself at home.

Vic goes off into the street. Gordon watches him go then moves round the back of the house and out of sight

Sylvia I thought Gordon was ever so brave last night.
Yvonne (*nervous, distracted*) Brave? Was he?
Sylvia Oh, yes. Standing up to his parents like that. Telling them about moving in with you, changing his job and everything. He doesn't want to be making deckchairs all his life, Yvonne.
Yvonne Jobs are not easy to get, though, Sylv. He shouldn't rush things.

Gordon appears at the frosted glass panel of the back door. Yvonne can see him but Sylvia can't. Gordon presses his face to the glass, trying to see through it

Yvonne (*seeing Gordon, in panic*) Sylvia, could you lend me something ...?
Sylvia Of course. What?
Yvonne Anything. Hairspray — that's it. I need some hairspray, don't I? There's a storm brewing outside.
Sylvia I'll have to go upstairs for it.
Yvonne Good. I mean ... good. (*She tries to smile*)
Sylvia (*heading for the hall*) Shan't be a minute.

Sylvia goes into the hall and up the stairs

Yvonne rushes and opens the back door

Gordon Have you told her ... ?
Yvonne I can't, Gordon. How can I?
Gordon It's my place to tell her, Yvonne. It's me who's been unfaithful.
Yvonne Well, I'd hardly call it that. I thought we'd agreed to look upon it only as a lesson, Gordon.
Gordon A lesson on how to feel good inside — I know. But lessons can be very boring, Yvonne. That wasn't. (*He attempts to kiss her*)
Yvonne Go away, Gordon. Leave it to me.

Sylvia comes downstairs again carrying a can of hairspray

Gordon Perhaps we shouldn't say anything. It might upset her.
Yvonne It's bound to upset her, you piecan! But you said you couldn't go through with it if we didn't tell her.
Gordon And you said you couldn't live with yourself if we didn't ...

Sylvia, passing the living-room, spots the wedding bouquets in the box. She goes in to look at them

Sylvia (*calling*) Oh, Yvonne ... have you seen our bouquets? They're beautiful ... (*She picks up one of the bouquets and heads for the kitchen*)
Yvonne (*to Gordon, whispering*) Go away — she's coming. (*Loudly to Sylvia*) Are they? How nice. (*To Gordon*) Hop it, Gordon — leave this to me.
Gordon Will you tell her?
Yvonne I'm not sure; I'll see how the land lies. (*She dismisses him with a gesture*)

Gordon goes, closing the door behind him

Sylvia (*entering the kitchen with the bouquet and hairspray*) This must be yours — it matches your dress, see. (*She gives the bouquet to Yvonne*)
Yvonne (*holding on to the back door*) Lovely, Sylv. What's yours like?

Act II, Scene 2   65

Sylvia Shall I show you? (*She leaves the kitchen again*)
Gordon (*opening the back door*) It's no good, Yvonne: I've got to be the one to tell her.

Sylvia picks up her own bouquet in the living-room and returns to the kitchen

Yvonne No, Gordon, it's me who's betrayed her. It's me who should tell her, now go away. (*She slams the kitchen door shut*)

Gordon peers through the frosted panel during the following

Sylvia (*coming into the kitchen*) See.
Yvonne Oh, lovely, Sylv.
Sylvia (*sitting at the table*) You know, Yvonne, I know I was the one who didn't want a big wedding — with all the trimmings and that — but I've got to confess I'm enjoying it now it's happening. The dress, the flowers ... (*She looks up and sees Gordon's face at the back door*) Oh, my God, Yvonne!
Yvonne What is it?
Sylvia There's a face at the window.
Yvonne (*white*) There isn't!
Sylvia It's all distorted, Yvonne. It could be Mum's pervert.
Yvonne Mum's pervert? Does Joyce know a pervert?
Sylvia My God — it's Gordon. Get rid of him, Yvonne. He mustn't see me before I get to the church. It's bad luck.
Gordon (*banging on the back door*) Sylvia, I must have a word with you, now, before we get married.
Sylvia (*rising, afraid*) You can't, Gordon. It's not allowed.
Yvonne Gordon, go away, will you?
Gordon I need to speak to you, Sylvia. We can't get married until I do.
Sylvia (*nervous, tearful*) He's starting again, Yvonne. The madness is returning. What shall I do?
Yvonne Go into the living-room, love — I'll try to get rid of him.
Sylvia (*running into the living-room*) Oh, why has life to be like this? Why can't everything be simple?

Sylvia enters the living-room and sits nervously at the table, bouquet in hand

Gordon pushes his way in past Yvonne who has been trying to keep him out

Gordon It's no use, Yvonne. I've got to tell her about last night. (*He calls loudly*) Sylvia, please listen to me.
Sylvia I can't see you, Gordon. I can't let you see me dressed like this. Our marriage is cursed if I show myself to you.

Yvonne You're raving mad, Gordon. You're like your father — you are.
Gordon (*at the kitchen door*) Look, I can talk from here. I needn't look at you.
Yvonne I give up. I'm sick of all this, Gordon.
Sylvia Is Yvonne there? Tell her to go away — then I'll talk to you from in here.

Gordon signals to Yvonne to leave

Gordon (*calling*) Yvonne's just leaving — aren't you, Yvonne? (*He lowers his voice*) Wait in the back yard.
Sylvia (*calling*) Has she gone?
Yvonne (*calling*) I'm just going, love. See you later. (*She lowers her voice*) Just be very careful, Gordon ... this fetish of yours for telling the truth worries me.

Yvonne exits out of the back door

Sylvia (*calling*) Has she gone?
Gordon (*sitting at the table, exhausted*) Yes, she's gone. (*To himself*) I'm knackered!

Silence. The rest of this scene is conducted with Sylvia and Gordon in separate rooms

Sylvia (*after a while*) Hallo, Gordon.
Gordon Hallo, Sylv.
Sylvia You sound as if you've become worked up again. Excitable.
Gordon Yes. (*He looks at the back door*) Very worked up!
Sylvia (*not hearing*) I'm sorry ... ?
Gordon (*louder*) No, I'm quite calm really — well, sort of. I just wanted to say thank you for telling me what you did last night.
Sylvia Thank you for taking it so well. I'd begun to dread telling you, Gordon.
Gordon It was very brave of you. Very open and honest.
Sylvia Well, we are committing ourselves for the rest of our lives.
Gordon Precisely. That's what I mean. It's a long time, Sylv.
Sylvia Sorry ... ?
Gordon Life's not going to be like our visits to the pictures now, you know. It's going to be a bit different from *Romeo and Juliet's*.
Sylvia Well, of course it is. I'm well aware of that. We're going to be together all the time. Night and day.
Gordon Every day, Sylv.

Sylvia (*modestly*) Yes, and every night as well.
Gordon (*awkwardly*) What if ... what if things didn't work out, Sylvia? What if things went wrong? Would we be able to manage, do you think?
Sylvia What things? (*A beat*) What things, Gordon?
Gordon Well, you know what I mean — life can be nasty sometimes — anything can crop up. Like that vicar said last week. Other women. Other men even.
Sylvia Don't be silly — why would I need another man? I seem to be having enough trouble getting you!
Gordon I know.
Sylvia I'm perfectly happy, Gordon. It is possible, you know. Look at your Mum and Dad — they've been happy all these years.

No answer

Gordon?
Gordon I'm listening. (*A beat*) Sylvia, you know what you said last night — about being honest? Well, that's what I want to be now.
Sylvia Oh, yes please — I want that, Gordon.
Gordon Mum and Dad parted company years ago. Oh, they live in the same house — eat the same food — even share the same bed. But they live like two snakes under a stone. They haven't any friends as such — no one ever knocks at our door or rings the bell. My dad gets up from a chair and immediately she straightens the cushions. As if to remove all trace of him.

Sylvia listens intently

Gordon And for quite a long time now, Dad has taken to seeking his pleasures elsewhere. Not that Mum seems to mind — in fact I often think she's happier when he's not there.
Sylvia Why are you telling me all this?
Gordon Because we've agreed to be honest, Sylv. What about your parents — what about Mr and Mrs Lomax — are they happy?
Sylvia I'm not sure. Perhaps not. Perhaps they never were. Who knows what would have happened if I hadn't turned up. Maybe, not being able to have children of their own, they might have split up — gone their separate ways.
Gordon And how does that affect you? Do you care?
Sylvia I'm not sure what you mean, Gordon.
Gordon My parents' way of life's affected me, Sylvia. So much so I sometimes think I'm like them. Dull, boring, incapable of love or feeling affection. Deceitful even.
Sylvia You're none of those things, Gordon.
Gordon How do you know? I could be deceitful.

Sylvia You don't tell lies. I know that.
Gordon All right — I don't tell lies — but that's not quite the same as not telling the truth.
Sylvia I'm not with you. I'm lost, Gordon.
Gordon Well, supposing I had a secret too. Something on my mind. Something which I might think would stand between us. It would be deceitful not to tell you, wouldn't it?
Sylvia I don't think so. Unless you've murdered somebody.

Yvonne enters again — Gordon signals her to go away

Yvonne (*sotto*) Have you told her?
Gordon (*sotto*) No. Go away.
Sylvia (*calling*) You haven't — have you?
Gordon (*calling*) Haven't what?
Sylvia Murdered someone.
Gordon No, of course I haven't!
Yvonne Don't tell her, Gordon. I couldn't bear it and what would be the point?
Sylvia (*calling*) This thing you're supposed to have done — is it so terrible?
Yvonne (*sotto*) No, Gordon. It isn't. It was meaningless.
Gordon (*calling, distracted now*) Perhaps not.
Sylvia Would it upset me — would it spoil the wedding?
Gordon It might. Yes, I suppose it would.
Yvonne (*sotto*) I'll never speak to you again, Gordon.
Gordon (*to Yvonne*) I couldn't bear that, Yvonne.
Yvonne I mean it, Gordon. Forget it. It's over.
Gordon It can't be. (*He rises*) I won't let it be over.
Sylvia What're you saying, Gordon — I can't hear you.
Gordon (*calling*) It might upset you. (*He closes in on Yvonne*)
Yvonne (*imploring him, sincere*) Please don't, Gordon.
Sylvia Then please don't tell me. Not today. I've had enough this week. Save it, Gordon. Tell me another time. (*A beat*) I love you, Gordon. (*Quietly now, almost to herself*) I love you.
Gordon (*looking into Yvonne's eyes, sincerely*) I love you.

Sylvia either doesn't catch his last remark or she simply can't believe that he's said it

Sylvia (*rising, bouquet in hand*) What did you say, Gordon?
Gordon (*to Yvonne*) I said ... I love you.

Gordon and Yvonne kiss passionately — long and hard. Both are so excited that they almost tear each other's clothes

Act II, Scene 2   69

Sylvia (*tears in her eyes, overjoyed*) Gordon. That's the very first time you've said it. You actually said it, Gordon.
Gordon (*pausing for breath, then loudly*) I love you!

They kiss again

Sylvia has tears streaming down her face

Joyce, Myrtle and Stanley come from the street into the garden

Joyce Just wait till our Sylvia sees that spread. (*She enters the house*) Sylv. You should see that wedding breakfast — it's astounding.
Sylvia (*calling to Gordon in panic*) Quick, Gordon! They're back — go out the back way!

Gordon and Yvonne leave quickly, hand in hand, out the back door, closing it after them

Joyce (*entering the living-room*) You'll get the surprise of your life, Sylv. Myrtle's a treasure — she is, Sylv — a real treasure! Thank God you chose Gordon, eh, love?
Sylvia Yes, Mum. Thank God.
Myrtle (*entering the living-room*) Well, I did it all for you, Sylvia. We always knew you were the right girl for our Gordon, didn't we, Stanley?
Stanley (*having entered the living-room*) Well, I had my reservations at first — you know that, Sylvia — and as I said to Yvonne last week — I think you're a very lucky young woman to be marrying our Gordon ...
Myrtle Stanley — don't start all that now ...
Stanley Just allow me to finish, Myrtle, please. But after Gordon's extremely odd behaviour all this week — and last night in particular — I just hope you know what you're taking on.

A moment — then he laughs — Myrtle laughs — then Joyce laughs

Sylvia (*almost in a trance, not listening to them*) Excuse me, Mr and Mrs Broadbent — Mum — I must just freshen my make-up.

Sylvia exits to the hall and up the stairs

Gordon and Yvonne, still hand in hand, come round from behind the house and into the garden

Joyce I think she's been having a little weep.
Myrtle Well, why not? It's a very emotional occasion, isn't it, Stan?

Stanley The poor girl's happy. Perhaps never be as happy again — who knows?
Yvonne (*in the garden*) Just go, Gordon. Before anybody sees you.
Gordon But when will I see you again?
Yvonne Don't be stupid — we'll meet in the church, won't we?
Gordon You know what I mean.
Yvonne Go, please. Go now.
Gordon Well, we are going to be living together, aren't we?

Yvonne gives Gordon a look

All right — I'm going.

He exits happily to the street

Yvonne (*pulling up her dress, smartening herself up, looking to heaven*) Oh, Sylvia, Sylvia — what have I done to you? (*She enters the house*) Anybody at home? I'm ready.

A car horn sounds in the street

Myrtle Oh, my God — that'll be Gordon's car — it's late.
Stanley Don't panic, Myrtle. Let's all keep calm.
Myrtle Yvonne — nip out and tell the driver that Gordon's over at your place — and, Yvonne ... ?
Yvonne Yes?
Myrtle Would you go with him? Make sure he gets to the church.
Yvonne Me?
Stanley It would be a good idea, Yvonne. Just in case — know what I mean.
Joyce (*with a little laugh*) Oh yes — we wouldn't want him changing his mind half-way there, would we?
Stanley And you can kiss the bridegroom in the car, Yvonne. (*With a dirty laugh*) It might be your last chance — eh, what?
Myrtle Now you see what my husband's like, Yvonne. That's men all over, dear.
Yvonne (*knowingly*) Yes. You don't have to tell me about men!

Sylvia comes downstairs again, carrying her make-up bag. She enters the living-room

Doesn't my friend looks gorgeous? I can't believe it's our little Sylvia. (*She kisses her on the cheek*) Good luck, love — I'll try and keep everything crossed!
Sylvia And you. And remember, Yvonne. Everything's going to be all right.

Act II, Scene 2   71

Yvonne smiles and runs out of the house and into the garden

Another car horn sounds in the street

Myrtle (*more panic*) Not our car, surely? (*She looks out of the window*) It is, you know. All my careful timing's going haywire, Stanley!

Yvonne comes out of the house

Vic comes into the garden from the street. He is looking rather thoughtful

Yvonne (*calling*) Hang on, Gordon — I'm coming with you — you're giving me a lift to the church!

Yvonne exits to the street

Vic (*calling after her*) Here — Yvonne ... !

Too late — she's gone — we hear a car driving away. Vic stands looking across at Yvonne's house

Stanley (*kissing Sylvia*) Just remember, Sylvia — if you can make our Gordon half as happy as I've made Myrtle you won't be doing so bad.
Sylvia I'll try, Mr Broadbent.
Myrtle Stanley, just stop spouting rubbish and go! Now, Mrs Lomax, Joyce, you're coming with us. Bye, Sylvia, love — I hope you've got that garter on for luck.
Sylvia Oh, no — I'll put it on now, Mrs Broadbent.
Myrtle "Mum" now remember. You've got two mums now, hasn't she, Joyce?
Joyce (*kissing Sylvia, tearful, sincere*) Oh, Sylv — what a day to remember, eh? It'll be a memory for evermore.
Sylvia Thanks, Mum. Thanks for everything you've ever done. (*During the following, she goes into the kitchen where she puts on the blue garter then attends to her make-up in the mirror*)
Myrtle (*coming out of the house with Stanley*) Now, don't forget — you're bringing your Sylvia, Mr Lomax.
Vic (*sitting on the wall now*) I'm not that daft, you know!
Stanley What was that, Lomax? (*He laughs*)

Stanley and Myrtle disappear into the street

Vic gives the Broadbents the "v" sign

Joyce (*coming out of the house*) Now, you look after that girl, Vic.
Vic Haven't I always?
Joyce Yes, well, we don't want a tragedy. See you in church — front pew — right hand side — or is it left?
Vic Just go, Joyce — go.
Joyce Here, you all right, Vic?
Vic (*deep in thought*) Eh? Oh, ay — I'm fine.

Joyce rushes out into the street as a car horn sounds. We hear the sound of car doors banging and a car driving off etc..

Vic stands for a moment in the garden, looking up at the ever-darker skies. There is another distant roll of thunder. Then Vic goes indoors, closing the front door behind him

Sylvia (*at the kitchen mirror*) Is that you, Dad?
Vic (*coming into the living-room, almost to himself*) Bloody fishy, if you ask me ...
Sylvia (*calling to him*) Well, Dad — it's the big day.
Vic (*sitting in his chair, talking to himself*) He must have slept with her ...
Sylvia (*putting make-up away in her bag*) There were times, Dad, when I didn't think we'd make it. Times when doubt began to creep in ...
Vic Bed unmade — his football togs strewn all over the place ...
Sylvia (*picking up her bouquet, smelling the flowers*) But here we are ... safe and sound. (*She leaves the kitchen and enters the living-room*) And I'm sorry it's costing such a lot, Dad — but we'll pay you back — every penny. That's what Gordon said too — last night — when I kissed him good-night outside Yvonne's ... (*She picks up the Valentine card and looks at it yet again*)
Vic Tea and toast they'd been having — and God knows what else ... !
Sylvia (*about the card*) I'm going to keep this for ever, Dad. My very first Valentine card.
Vic The spare room hadn't even been slept in.
Sylvia Sorry ... ?

A car horn sounds out in the street

Sylvia (*excited*) The car, Dad — it's the car.
Vic Sylvia ...
Sylvia (*smiling, happy, taking his arm*) Yes, Dad?
Vic (*thinking better of it*) Oh, never mind ... it'll keep.

Thunder, nearer now, rolls again and the Lights slowly fade to Black-out

CURTAIN

FURNITURE AND PROPERTY LIST

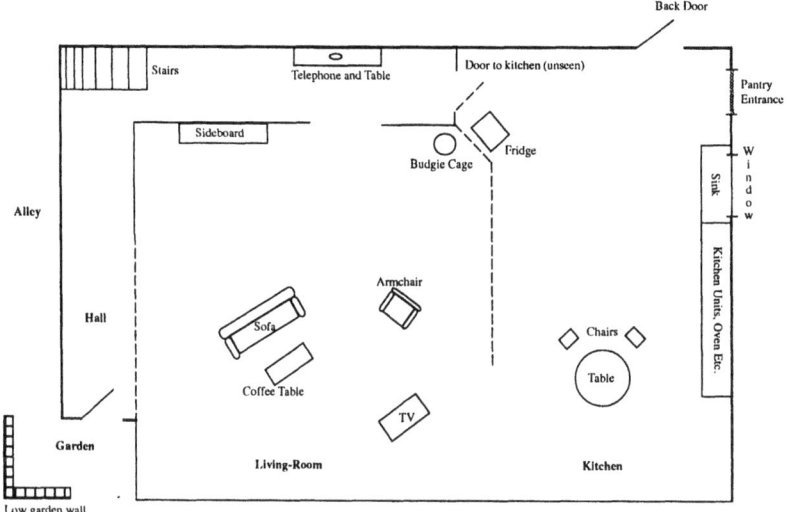

Dotted lines indicate cutaway walls

ACT I
Scene 1

On stage: Hall
Small table. *On it*: telephone

Living-Room
Sofa
Coffee table
Armchair
TV set
Budgie cage. *In it*: "budgie"
Cover for budgie cage with "Hoppy" embroidered on it
Paperback books

KITCHEN
Sink with practical taps
Kitchen units. *In them*: tin of biscuits, box of bird seed, black plastic bin-liner, coffee, tea, shoe polish and cloth
Oven
Fridge. *In it*: bottle of milk, carton of orange juice
Table
Chairs
Cups and saucers
Glasses
Kettle (practical)
Tray
Sugar bowl
Teapot
Napkins

Off stage: Umbrella (**Yvonne**)
Valentine card, umbrella (**Sylvia**)

Personal: **Joyce**: bottle of tablets
Sylvia: front door key

SCENE 2

Re-set: Tea things
Orange juice glass
Cover on budgie cage

Set: LIVING ROOM
Packet of crisps for **Yvonne**
Pins and tape measure for **Myrtle**
Myrtle's handbag. *In it*: sheets of paper with lists on them, pen

Strike: **Vic**'s newspaper

Off stage: Bucket containing ball cock, tool chest (**Stanley**)
Shopping trolley, bags of shopping, including cuttlefish bone, tin of salmon (**Joyce**)
Chips wrapped in newspaper (**Sylvia** and **Gordon**)
Letter (**Vic**)

Personal: **Stanley**: bill
Joyce: keys

ACT II
Scene 1

Set:	Living-Room Black cloth on budgie cage Wedding presents including gas stove with ribbon and card tied around it
Strike:	Tea things
Personal:	**Sylvia**: handkerchief

Scene 2

Set:	Pair of ladies' shoes in a box for **Joyce** **Sylvia**'s Valentine card
Off stage:	Box of carnations, two bouquets (**Myrtle**) **Gordon**'s suit and top hat (**Stanley**) Hairbrush (**Yvonne**) Can of hairspray (**Sylvia**) Make-up bag (**Sylvia**)
Personal:	**Myrtle**: handbag containing blue garter and cross and chain

LIGHTING PLOT

Practical fittings required: TV flicker effect, living-room central light fitting
Three interiors, hall, living-room and kitchen with exterior backing to garden window. One exterior: front door and garden. The same throughout

ACT I, SCENE 1

To open: Street lamp effect on front garden exterior

Cue 1	**Yvonne** disappears round the side of the house *Slowly bring up practicals in the living-room with general cover and TV flicker effects*	(Page 1)
Cue 2	**Yvonne** enters the kitchen *Bring up lights on kitchen*	(Page 1)
Cue 3	**Joyce** switches off the TV *Cut flicker effect*	(Page 2)
Cue 4	**Yvonne** and **Sylvia** head for the kitchen *Fade lights on garden*	(Page 6)
Cue 5	**Joyce** switches on the TV *Bring up flicker effect*	(Page 10)
Cue 6	**Joyce** and **Vic** fall silent *Bring up light on garden*	(Page 10)
Cue 7	**Vic** turns off the TV *Cut flicker effect*	(Page 14)
Cue 8	**Myrtle**: "He'll go to Skegness once too often ..." *Fade lights slightly on living-room and bring lights up more intensely on kitchen*	(Page 19)
Cue 9	**Sylvia**: "Oh, yes, Gordon, I will marry you." *Bring up lights on living-room*	(Page 21)
Cue 10	**Vic**: "God help us!" *Fade all lights*	(Page 21)

Sylvia's Wedding

ACT I, Scene 2

To open: Bright lights on entire stage except living-room practicals

Cue 11	**Vic** sinks on to the wall *Slowly fade lights to black-out*	(Page 37)

ACT II, Scene 1

To open: Darkness. When ready, bring up:
    (a) spot on bird cage
    (b) spot on **Vic**'s armchair
    (c) street lamp effect on front garden
    (d) living-room lights, practicals with cover

Cue 12	**Sylvia** goes into the kitchen *Bring up lights on kitchen*	(Page 39)
Cue 13	**Yvonne** enters the kitchen *Cross-fade lights from living-room to kitchen*	(Page 41)
Cue 14	**Sylvia**: "Will he ever come back?" *Cross-fade lights from kitchen to living-room*	(Page 42)
Cue 15	**Vic** switches on the TV *Bring up TV flicker effect*	(Page 45)
Cue 16	**Vic** switches off the TV *Cut TV flicker effect*	(Page 46)
Cue 17	**Yvonne** goes of into the street *Fade lights on the garden and kitchen*	(Page 52)
Cue 18	**Gordon** and **Sylvia** settle back on the sofa. Music *Fade lights to black-out*	(Page 53)

ACT II, Scene 2

To open: General interior lighting without practicals; gloomy, overcast effect on front garden and exterior backing, fading throughout the scene

Cue 19	Thunder rolls again *Slowly fade lights to black-out*	(Page 72)

EFFECTS PLOT

ACT I

Cue 1	As play begins *Rain effect*	(Page 1)
Cue 2	Lights come up slowly on living-room *Bring up TV sound*	(Page 1)
Cue 3	**Joyce** switches off the TV *Cut TV sound*	(Page 2)
Cue 4	**Stanley** rings the doorbell *Loud doorbell*	(Page 11)
Cue 5	**Vic** turns the TV sound up *Increase volume of TV sound; football crowd roar*	(Page 13)
Cue 6	**Vic** turns the sound down *Decrease volume of TV sound*	(Page 13)
Cue 7	**Vic**: "God help us!" *Music; cut rain effect*	(Page 21)
Cue 8	As Scene 2 begins *Fade music*	(Page 21)
Cue 9	**Vic**: "New ball cock and bits — what's this?" *Noise of Gordon attempting to flush the lavatory*	(Page 36)

ACT II

Cue 10	**Sylvia** sighs deeply *Telephone rings*	(Page 38)
Cue 11	**Gordon** and **Sylvia** settle back on the sofa *Music*	(Page 53)
Cue 12	As Scene 2 begins *Distant roll of thunder*	(Page 53)
Cue 13	**Vic**: "And it's costing the earth!" *Distant rumble of thunder*	(Page 55)

Sylvia's Wedding

Cue 14	**Gordon** dodges round the side of the house *Roll of thunder — nearer*	(Page 61)
Cue 15	**Yvonne**: "I'm ready." *Car horn*	(Page 70)
Cue 16	**Yvonne** runs into the garden *Car horn*	(Page 71)
Cue 17	**Vic**: "Here — Yvonne ... !" *Sound of a car driving off*	(Page 71)
Cue 18	**Vic**: "Oh ay — I'm fine." *Car horn; then sounds of car doors banging, car driving off*	(Page 72)
Cue 19	**Vic** looks up at the sky *Another distant roll of thunder*	(Page 72)
Cue 20	**Sylvia**: "Sorry ... ?" *Car horn*	(Page 72)
Cue 21	**Vic**: "Oh, never mind ... it'll keep." *Thunder — nearer now*	(Page 72)

A licence issued by Samuel French Ltd to perform this play does not include permission to use the Incidental music specified in this copy. Where the place of performance is already licensed by the PERFORMING RIGHT SOCIETY a return of the music used must be made to them. If the place of performance is not so licensed then application should be made to the Performing Right Society, 29 Berners Street, London W1.

www.ingramcontent.com/pod-product-compliance
Ingram Content Group UK Ltd.
Pitfield, Milton Keynes, MK11 3LW, UK
UKHW021844210426
5322IPUK00022B/460